RUBBER STAMPING
ARTIST TRADING CARDS

TWEETYJILL PUBLICATIONS

Acknowledgements

Rubber Stamping Artist Trading Cards
Second printing 2008
Copyright by TweetyJill Publications, Inc.

Published and created by:
TweetyJill Publications, Inc.
5824 Bee Ridge Road
PMB 412
Sarasota, FL 34233

For information about wholesale, please contact
Customer Service at www.tweetyjill.com or 1-800-595-5497.
Ask for free flyer detailing all TweetyJill Publication, Inc. craft titles.
Printed in China
ISBN 1-891898-11-6 • 978-1-891898-11-2

Book Design: Laurie Doherty

Book Layout: Jill Haglund

Managing Editor: Lisa Codianne Fowler

Associate Editors: Carlene Federer;
Marla Neuf

Photography: Herb Booth of
Herb Booth Studios, Inc.,
Sarasota, FL

Photo Stylist: Jill Haglund

Table of Contents

ABCDEFG H
MNOPQRSTU
XYZ123456789
QUEENS

EXOTIC

123456789

②

man (noun)
1. an adult male
human being
6. a husband, lover,
or sweetheart

9

C
CIRCLES

love me

sweetheart

PRICELES
00000 00000

Art is Love

It was hardly wise to taunt him

A Joyful spirit
is evidence of
a grateful
heart.

123
456

THINK
OUTSIDE
THE BOX

arefree

ARTIST TRADING CARDS
are your own miniature works of art, no larger than a playing card!

No you don't sell them; and you don't buy others. YOU ONLY TRADE THEM... hence the name! ATCs are all the rage. YOU need to catch the wave and have fun! This book not only makes it easy but also adds an exciting twist to this incredibly popular art form. Rubber Stamping Artist Trading Cards features the classic 2 ½" x 3 ½" pocket-sized "canvas," but each and every little ATC is created using one or more rubber stamps!

Designed to be an artist calling card, ATCs are flexible and addictive! Due to their size, they allow for trying new techniques. One can spend as little or as much time as desired creating them. We have arty, funky, sophisticated, bright and cheerful, edgy- every style imaginable for you to dabble in at your leisure.

If you're a seasoned stamper, you will delight in discovering new and creative ways to use your existing rubber stamps. You'll also have a great excuse to purchase new images... the ones you've wanted but weren't sure how you would use them. You will be inspired as you peruse the astonishing variety of cards. The materials list for each provides the name of the stamp companies, and a handy resource guide at the end of the book gives you their websites.

If you're NEW to the idea of Artist Trading Cards you no longer need to be intimidated! You will see each card in detail; many have step-by-step instructions or fresh illustrated techniques that are easy to follow. You'll learn everything you need to know to get started right away. We even offer an extensive list of online ATC groups - there's a big world of small art out there!

You'll have fun designing these tiny treasures. Remember, trading them, and the size are the only rules; creating them is left to your imagination. Let it fly! This book will show you how.

A "Little" History

Once upon a time in a land faraway, artists painted in miniature. The tiny canvases, created in 16th century Europe, were true works of art. But they also served a practical purpose. They were mostly portraits, and they were sold, not traded or given away and could actually be considered the first "wallet-sized" photos! Wealthy men commissioned paintings of their mistresses in the nude, the small format allowed them to keep the pictures discretely hidden. Miniature portraits were also used as an introduction during match making. This caused a big problem for Henry the Eighth, when the artist who painted his fourth wife-to-be portrayed her as "slightly" more attractive. A face-to-face meeting inspired Henry to leave her. (Interesting. Sounds like ancient thinking, but consider today's digitally enhanced photos and Internet dating services...)

Miniature art cards were also used for advertising, first by the French, and then by the English in the mid-1700s. By the 20th century Impressionist painters began trading their original art among themselves to study each other's styles and techniques. They also traded or sold them for income during hard times, affording them art supplies, food and lodging.

In the meantime, back in the good ol' U.S.A, baseball became a beloved sport and baseball cards began to appear in the mid-1800s. They were not mass-produced and not for trade or sale but rather mementos of a great game or favorite team or player. By the 1900s, thanks to the Industrial Revolution, they were mass-produced and often sold with bubble gum, chewing tobacco and Cracker Jacks. The cards varied in size according to the product with which they were marketed. It was not until the 1960s that the 2 ½ " x 3 ½ " size became standard.

Fast forward to 1997. The standard-sized baseball card had found its way to a variety of sports and games, and cards were passionately traded by both adults and children. Enter "The Father of ATCs", M. Vanci Stirnemann. Inspired by hockey trading cards, the Swiss artist created and showcased 1,200 similarly-sized cards, his original works of art, in his gallery in Zurich, Switzerland. He told people who wanted one of his cards to come back and bring one of their own in trade.

Stirnemann's work spread to Canada through Calgary artist Don Mabie (a.k.a. Chuck Stake), who had visited the Zürich show and participated in a 1997 trading session. In 2000, the two collaborated on an exhibition, "The First International Biennial of Artist Trading Cards" in Calgary, Canada with 80 artists from ten different countries. The concept had caught on like wildfire across the globe. And the rest, as they say, is history!

Getting Started with Materials & Tools

Wood or Acrylic Mounted Rubber Stamps

It is exciting to go into a craft or rubber stamp store and see the wall lined with images that inspire! What to buy? What to use on your next Artist Trading Card! You can choose any stamp that strikes your fancy or catches your eye to be part of your Artist Trading Card creation. There are a multitude of stamps that are adhered to wood or acrylic blocks with the image represented on top.

Unmounted Rubber Stamp Plates

Unmounted stamps need to be adhered to a special adhesive foam and then cut out with scissors made for cutting rubber. You need to cut as close to the image as possible without cutting into it. You can purchase acrylic blocks in different dimensions specifically made for the unmounted stamps to fit onto for stamping. Check with the retailer or manufacturer of rubber stamp plates regarding detailed instructions for cutting rubber images, purchase of special scissors to cut rubber adhered to foam and precise storage of ummounted stamps.

Playing Cards

Pick a card, any card. Really! A wonderful and easy way to begin creating an ATC is to use a baseball card or a playing card from a deck. It's incredibly convenient… not only is it already the proper size, but it also provides a sturdy, solid base on which to work. To begin a background for your ATC, simply paint, color or adhere plain or patterned paper directly onto the playing card front. Then just trim any edges as necessary with scissors.

Adhesives

You can adhere papers with a glue stick and smooth them with a bone folder to insure flat drying. A small glue stick works well for securing cut and torn papers that seem to flip up or hard to reach areas.

Another choice is the Xyron 500 machine. It is the perfect size to run a playing card through to apply adhesive before adding torn or cut papers.

JudiKins is an absolutely fabulous, versatile adhesive for gluing almost anything three-dimensional, such as rhinestones, sequins, buttons, leaves, transparencies and trim.

Foam tape is a great product for providing dimension to areas of your work. If you have a heavy, bulky piece you want to add, try E-6000; make sure you are in a well-ventilated area when using this adhesive and let dry overnight before handling.

We recommend you experiment and select adhesives you like to use most.

Tools

Here you see most tools you will need to reproduce the techniques used throughout this book; most you likely already own. A papercutter and/or scissors are used frequently, therefore we do not list them in the Tools section of the Materials for each ATC. Some tools are used only once in awhile, such as a brayer, stapler, a heat tool for embossing, both clear acyrlic and metal edge rulers for measuring and tearing papers and an eyelet setting tool and punches.

There are a variety of tools for setting eyelets. The new Crop-A-Dile shown above by We R Memories is convenient because it punches two sizes of holes and sets two sizes of eyelets, plus sets snaps - and does it all silently and effortlessly.

A bone folder, shown to the right, is a must-have to smooth your work as you adhere and layer papers or cut images to your cards. A bone folder decreases any chance for bubbles or wrinkles once dry.

Embellishments and Ephemera

Although our ATCs focus on rubber stamped images, we could not resist using ephemera, goodies, stuff, doodads, embellishments - whatever you like to call them - to make these cards even jazzier. You'll see torn old papers, stamps, cancelled postage on envelopes, tags, tickets, illustrations, numbers, glitter, ribbons, fibers, lace, buttons, brads, eyelets and trims to name a few... and so much more!

As you flip through these pages filled with hundreds of ATCs created by dozens of artists, you will see they have liberally added their very own favorite things. Feel free to add yours!

All About Inkpads

Each type of ink has specific qualities and works better for different stamping techniques than other inks might. Below is a list of ink types, their properties and how you can best use them.

MEMORIES DYE INKPADS: Memories dye-based inks are fade resistant, embossable and water resistant. They are permanent inks and give a sharp, crisp image.

STAZON: StazOn is acid-free, archival, fast-drying solvent ink appropriate for all surfaces. It is one of the few inks that is well suited for stamping fine, detailed images on glossy cardstock.

VERSAFINE: A natural oil-based ink that dries instantly on matte cardstock. VersaFine, as its name implies, is ideal for fine detail. It can be watercolored or markered over without bleeding. Although it's oil-based it cleans up easily with water and actually conditions the rubber on your stamp.

VERSAMARK WATERMARK: A versatile ink that allows you to perform a number of amazing techniques. Stamp your image onto text-weight paper to explore the possibilities of watermarking, or stamp subtle tone-on-tone images onto colored cardstock. Create a resist image by stamping on glossy and brayering with dye ink. VersaMark is sticky and acts as a "glue" for chalks and pigment powders.

INDIA INK BLACK: A permanent acid-free, waterproof, fade-resistant, super-fast drying formula for use on porous and non-porous surfaces. Because of these qualities, it's non-smudging and non-bleeding and is excellent for use with watercolors, watercolor pencils, markers and blending pastels.

KALEIDACOLOR: Twenty striking rainbow combinations that stay vibrant and clean due to a special patented sliding palette; slide the palette together to stamp and slide it apart to store.

Note: Waterproof inks are necessary to use if you are going to apply ANY water to the image in the form of watercolors, Twinkling H2Os, paints or oil pastels. They resist all water and will not bleed.

Color Box and Memories Pigment and Chalk Inks

Pigment-based inks are water-soluble, slower drying and resist fading even in sunlight, unlike dye-based inks. They are vibrant in intensity and appear the same color they stamp out. They work well for embossing paper, fabric and even wood. On glossy stock these inks must be embossed otherwise they may never dry. Pigments can be mixed to create new colors, but they do not form a solution with water like dyes. For this reason, the colors do not bleed into one another in multicolored stamp pads. Pigment inks need to be heat set or embossed to dry.

Fluid Chalk Pigment inks are wonderful for rubbing directly onto your paper's front or edge for color.

BRILLIANCE: Fast-drying ink in rich pearlescent colors. Designed for use on shiny papers, Brilliance dries well on vellum, mica, acetate, photo papers, sculpting clay, shrink plastic and more. Because it dries so quickly, smudging is never an issue.

DISTRESS INKS: Acid-free, fade resistant, water-based dye inks that are perfect for achieving a vintage, stained or aged look to paper and cardstock. Available in a myriad of colors, the raised inkpad makes it perfect for the direct-to-paper technique. Crumble paper, rub inks onto surface, spray with a mist of water and iron flat for great backgrounds.

Ink colors and brands are listed throughout the book; brands and manufacturers can be found in the Shopping and Resource Guides on pages 158-159.

Cosmetic Sponges, triangular rubber makeup sponges and stipple brushes are fabulous for applying inks directly to the paper. See techinque on page 21.

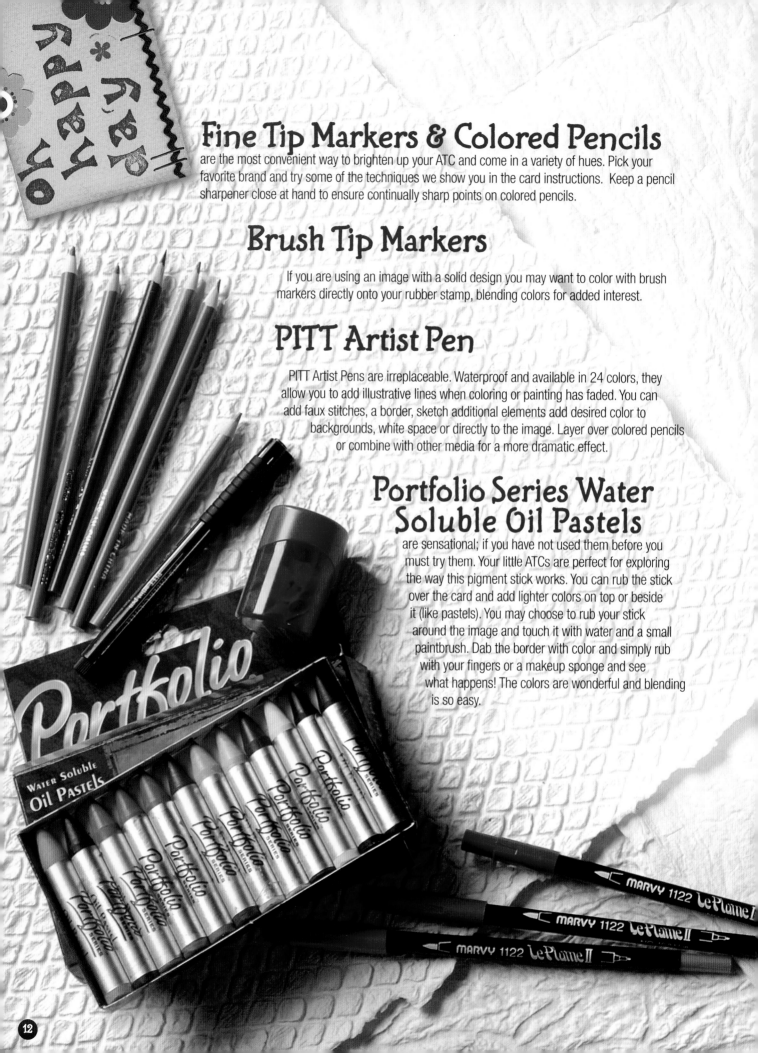

Fine Tip Markers & Colored Pencils

are the most convenient way to brighten up your ATC and come in a variety of hues. Pick your favorite brand and try some of the techniques we show you in the card instructions. Keep a pencil sharpener close at hand to ensure continually sharp points on colored pencils.

Brush Tip Markers

If you are using an image with a solid design you may want to color with brush markers directly onto your rubber stamp, blending colors for added interest.

PITT Artist Pen

PITT Artist Pens are irreplaceable. Waterproof and available in 24 colors, they allow you to add illustrative lines when coloring or painting has faded. You can add faux stitches, a border, sketch additional elements add desired color to backgrounds, white space or directly to the image. Layer over colored pencils or combine with other media for a more dramatic effect.

Portfolio Series Water Soluble Oil Pastels

are sensational; if you have not used them before you must try them. Your little ATCs are perfect for exploring the way this pigment stick works. You can rub the stick over the card and add lighter colors on top or beside it (like pastels). You may choose to rub your stick around the image and touch it with water and a small paintbrush. Dab the border with color and simply rub with your fingers or a makeup sponge and see what happens! The colors are wonderful and blending is so easy.

Watercolor
Pencils are different from regular
colored pencils; color your ATC or images in desired
areas and touch them with a small paintbrush with a little
water, and more intense colors bloom right before your eyes.
They are good used alone or to enhance colored pencils or
watercolors for shadows or highlights.

Watercolors

Many ATCs in this book use watercolors. You can achieve any color
you wish by mixing watercolors if you know the basics. Make sure you
don't make "mud". You may want to pick up a simple book on watercolor
techniques to help you get going. Use wide brush for backgrounds and
small brush for images. Let one color dry before adding another, otherwise
your miniature will have all the colors running together... not a pretty picture!

Twinkling H2O's are a new addition to the color scene.
If you have trouble finding them at your local craft store, try a framing and fine arts
store. They come in little pots of striking colors! Read the directions for these paints;
you must add a little water and wait a few minutes to get the colors juicy and ready
to work for you. Twinkling H2O's add a beautiful shimmer to your ATC that no
other medium can; try them and see. You can add a little luster over markers,
colored pencils, oil pastels or watercolors. Beware -- they are addictive! (Make
sure you store with lids tight to avoid a colorful disaster!)

Acrylic Paints

Acrylic Paints in any color or brand add a nice texture and touch of color to the
edges of ATCs. Acrylics are used for the "dry brush" technique where you apply
a small amount of paint to a bristle brush and drag it across the paper, leaving a
scant amount of paint in its path.

Brushes

Keep a good supply of brushes on hand. Use wide and flat brushes for washes and a
small tip brush for detail work. Use a bristle brush for dry brushing acrylics or edging ATCs.

There are many creative avenues to choose from when adding color to
your card and/or stamped image. The best part is that you never need
to be shy about experimenting! Just explore our mixed media
techniques and discover how to use products alone or together.

Refer to our Shopping and Resource Guides at the
back of the book for brands and manufacturer websites.

STAMPING BASICS

When you begin to stamp Artist Trading Cards it will help you to have a few stamping basics, tips and techniques under your belt to encourage success. Here we dedicate a section chock full of exactly that to get you off on the right foot. If your stamping ability is beyond basic, please feel free to refresh yourself and read through to the more complex techniques to ensure your understanding. If you are a seasoned stamper... go straight to the ATC section for inspiration!

Foam Rubber Stamp Pads

For all your stamping work use a rubber pad as your surface. These pads are made especially for rubber stamping and are sold at craft and stamp stores.

Applying Ink to Stamps

If your stamp image is large, flip the stamp over and press the pad onto the stamp to achieve full ink coverage. Visually check to make sure it is completely inked.

Smaller images can be pressed with equal pressure directly onto the pad.

It is important to apply pressure evenly. If you have never stamped, practice. Don't push too hard on the pad or ink will seep into undesired details of the stamp image and result in an undefined impression. If you press too gently you will get a weak impression. Strive for crisp detail and deep color from your stamped image.

TIP:
Do not "rock" stamp or your image will blur.

Applying Pressure to Paper

Once the image is inked you are ready to stamp on paper. As you stamp make sure you apply equal pressure firmly across entire surface to capture the image details.

Playing Card Preparation (Optional)

Most playing cards and some baseball cards have a semi-gloss face surface. For better paper adhesion and/or paint coverage, you may either apply gesso to the surface or sand the card.

Gesso

Apply white gesso to the face of each card you want to cover with paper. Gesso gives a matte finish that allows for easy adhesion of papers to surface.

Sandpaper

Sanding the card face lightly with fine-grit sandpaper will diminish the gloss and allow paper adhesives to do their job!.

Cleaning Stamps

Your rubber stamps will last almost indefinitley if you take care of them. Protect them from excess heat or cold temperatures, and make sure your stamps are clean when you store them. This allows fine image detail for future stamping without an ink build-up on the rubber surface.

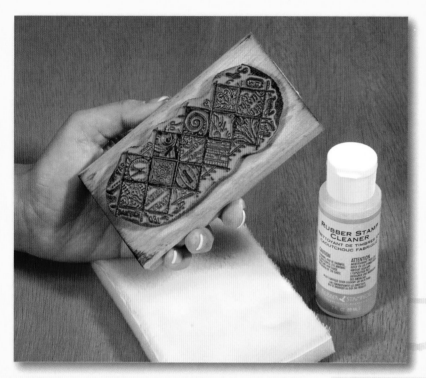

STEP ONE:

It is easy to remove residual ink from your stamps. Rubber Stampede Stamp and Scrub Cleaning Pad and Cleaner combination is quick and tidy. First, rinse pad under running water to remove excess fibers. Allow to dry.

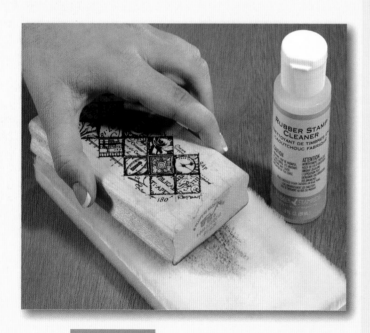

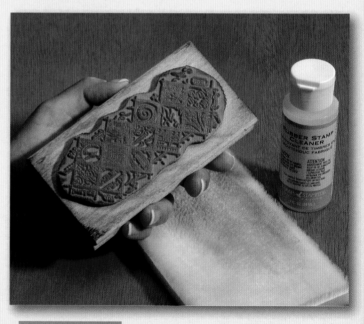

STEP TWO:

Clean stamp gently by rubbing across fiber surface. Be careful not to "spray" your surroundings.

STEP THREE:

Once stamp is clean, blot on a paper towel. After use, rinse cleaning pad under running water to remove ink. Allow to dry.

Stamp Positioner

Stamp positioners are handy tools that facilitate stamp placement. Once you become adept at using one, you will find it invaluable.

The following instructions are for the Stamp-a-ma-jig by EK Success. Follow the steps and practice to take advantage of this user-friendly tool.

STEP ONE:

Stamp first image onto cardstock.

STEP TWO:

Position blank image sheet tightly in the the corner of the Stamp-a-ma-jig and stamp the image you wish to align.

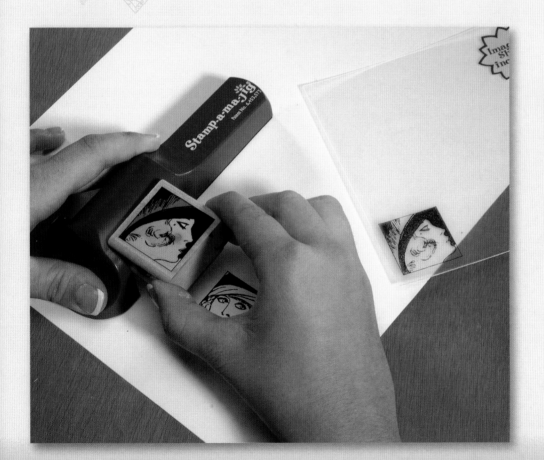

STEP THREE:

Position stamped image sheet on cardstock in desired location. Make sure it is securly in the corner of Stamp-a-ma-jig. Once positioned, slowly remove image sheet and stamp image.

STAMPING TECHNIQUES

Direct-to-Paper

This technique has been around a long time and is a classic way to add color to the surface or edges of paper.

You may use any type ink pad; try different ones to see the versatile effects. You can also use a variety of tools such as different types of sponges, a ColorBox Stylus or a stipple brush.

One method is to simply rub the inkpad directly onto the ATC edge or front. Practice on scrap pieces of cardstock and papers to the see the effects of different ink types, colors and inkpad shapes. Feel comfortable with it so that when you reach for a pad you know what the result will be.

Materials:

Rubber Stamp, pigment or dye inks and ColorBox Stylus tool (one for each color). Tools for applying inks are actually optional; you may want to rub the inkpad directly onto paper or cardstock.

TIP:

As you apply inks directly to the paper, visualize the end result so you can place the colors in the areas you want. It takes practice if you want the image to look a specific way (see step 2). Alternately, you can just blend colors and stamp without a predetermined color scheme.

STEP ONE:

We chose to use a Clearsnap's Stylus tool to blend juicy pigment inks onto the paper for more control of ink flow. Reapply for more intensity. Let dry or dry with a heat tool.

STEP TWO:

Stamp image onto blended and dried inks.

Masking the Positive Image

Masking is an important basic you that you need to practice and master. It allows you to add a design in the background area without stamping on top of your original rubber stamped image. This technique opens up a whole new world of stamping and gives you license to create unlimited designs by combining images.

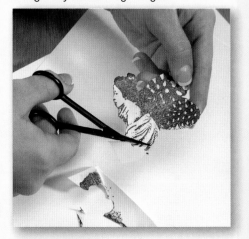

STEP ONE:

Here we chose to use the Asian ATC again to show you how we combine techniques. Make a mask by stamping another image of the Asian Girl onto a Post-it Note; carefully cut it out.

STEP TWO:

Lay mask on top of image. Once in place, get ready to stamp.

STEP THREE:

Stamp over image with second design. In this instance, it is flowers in red ink.

STEP FOUR:

Lift the mask. The second stamped image will appear only in the background once masks are removed.

STEP FIVE :

Enhance image with colored pencils.

Color Applied Directly onto Stamp with Brush Marker

The bamboo tree is a solid design and works well to demonstrate applying and blending color with brush markers directly to stamp.

STEP ONE:

Start with one section at a time and work quickly, but carefully. You want the inks to stay as wet as possible. Color bamboo branch with light brown first, then edge with dark brown. Two shades of brown blend well on the finished image. Before brown ink dries, apply green directly on the leaf part of the stamp image.

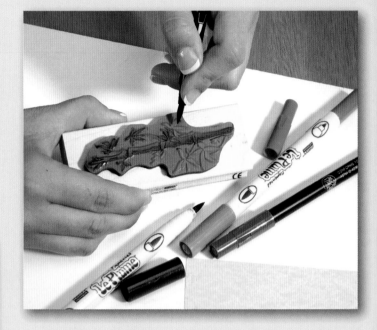

STEP TWO:

Hold the inked, stamped image approximately one inch out from your mouth and breathe out slowly to add a little moisture to ink. Stamp onto cardstock.

Voila!

Dry Brush Technique

Here is a simple demonstration of using the dry brush technique on regular paper. You can use any type brush you desire. In our steps we have used a bristle brush.

Materials:

All you need is paper, acrylic paint, a brush and water.

STEP ONE:

Dip brush into acrylic paint. Once you achieve a consistency you like, apply paint with light strokes to paper's edge. Practice makes perfect! Explore how your paints and brushes react to different textures.

STEP TWO:

Add another shade of paint or additional paint colors. Let dry in between each color.

Finished ATC

Masking the Negative Image

This technique requires patience, but it is worth mentioning because it creates a unique effect: the image appears to be snuggled into the background because it is slightly recessed.

STEP ONE:

Stamp the image twice, once on the paper you choose as the background and once on the cardstock you will use as the base.

STEP TWO:

Cut out image stamped onto the background. Start by cutting into the image itself and cutting it out. Do not cut into paper intended for background of ATC.

STEP THREE:

When you are done, you should have a perfect shape of the image outline cutout.

STEP FOUR:

Color your image that is stamped on the cardstock before adhereing the negative mask on top. For a bright, colorful effect use Water Soluble Oil pastels. Color image and blend with water to soften the effect.

STEP FIVE:

Layer cut out negative mask over colored image with glue.

Chalk Resist

To softly blend colors, experiment with the chalk resist technique. VersaMark WaterMark is an excellent choice of embossing pad because it creates an adhesive surface that chalks cling to.

STEP ONE:

Use stamp positioner to stamp images on cardstock and on a Post-it Note.

STEP TWO:

Cut out the images stamped on Post-it-Note to make masks.

STEP THREE:

Mask mages and stamp desired background image in VersaMark WaterMark inkpad or any embossing pad. Let set two minutes or dry with heat tool.

STEP FOUR:

Color background image gently with chalks using applications.

STEP FIVE:

Remove masks.

STEP SIX:

Color remaining images and spray with a fixative to set and keep from smudging.

One second
One minute
One hour
One day

Stipple Brush used with Masks and Stencils

Another method of applying inks is with a tool called a stipple brush. You can use this technique simply for the general effect or use masks like stencils (shown below).

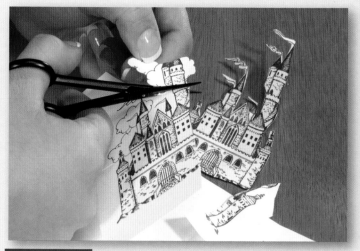

STEP ONE:

In this pariculiar project the first step is to stamp two images. The first image is cut out for coloring.

STEP TWO:

The second image is used as the cloud stencil. Cut around clouds as shown.

STEP THREE:

Layer cloud stencil behind and stipple by dabbing your stipple brush onto the inkpad color(s). Next, "pounce" brounce brush in a straight up and down motion onto cardstock to get the stippled effect.

STEP FOUR:

Adhere stamped and colored castle image over stippling. Glue to prepared playing card and trim.

You may want to try stippling the outer edge with less ink on the brush and increasing the color and pressure as you go toward the center of the ATC. Experiment with mixing your inks to see how the stippling technique works for you.

Twinkling H2O's

There's more than a pot of gold at the end of this rainbow of colors. These little pots of paints have a wonderful shimmer once dry. Just open, add a wet paint brush and use them right out of the pot - once used, tightly replace lid. The next time you use them you may have to spritz or add a half teaspoon of water to each one and let set a few minutes to get the proper consistency.

Materials:

Rubber stamp, waterproof inkpad, Twinkling H2O's, small paint brush and bowl of water.

STEP ONE:

Dip brush in water and then into paint. Water will give you control over the color value. The paints blend nicely and work well on fine detail.

Finished ATC

Embossing

Embossing is addictive! All it takes is one special embossing pad, embossing powder and a heat tool to get you started. Embossing powders come in four weights: detail, regular, thick and ultra thick.

Materials:

Rubber stamp, cardstock, detail embossing powder, heat tool and an inkpad especially made for embossing such as VersaMark WaterMark.

STEP ONE:

Stamp image onto paper with embossing pad.

STEP TWO:

Sprinkle embossing powder in your choice of colors onto wet embossed image before it dries.

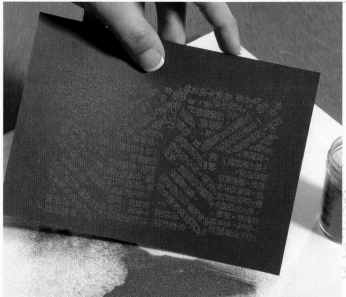

STEP THREE:

Shake off powder onto paper.

STEP FOUR:

Once powder is on image, you have plently of time to emboss. A good rule to follow is to fold paper like a funnel and add the excess embossing powder you shook off back to jar and cap tightly before continuing. Few things are more messy then a a tipped over bottle of embossing powder.

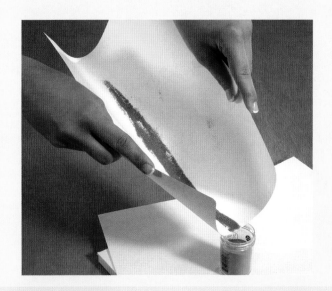

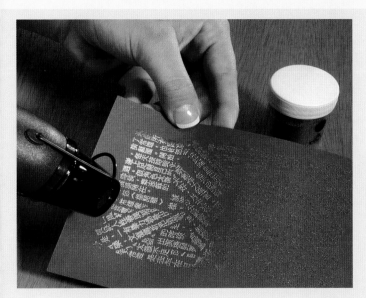

STEP FIVE:

During this procedure it is essential to keep your fingers clear of heat tool tip as it gets extrememly hot. Hold the heat tool half way up the handle and switch on.

Direct tip approximately one inch away from paper towards powder. Slowly move tool and watch carefully to ensure complete embossing. Powder should appear to melt before your eyes giving it an enamel-like appearance.

Let cool 10 seconds and check the image with your fingers to make sure it is totally embossed with no dry embossing powders in sight. If there are any particles left, just emboss again until completed.

Embossing powders or mica pigments are available in a wide range of colors. Gold, silver and copper are the most popular. When embossing with a clear embossing pad, such as VersaMark WaterMark, sprinkle on any colored powders to get your desired effect.

Or you may use colored pigment inks and sprinkle clear embossing powder to achieve the colored image. Clear embossing powder can be used with all inks.

Finished ATC

BOX ONE *Amy Wellenstein*

1. Photocopy and trace box illustration onto white cardstock, or trace a flattened box from a deck of playing cards. Cut out the box.
2. Score along all fold lines using a bone folder.
3. Stamp desired focal image onto the box front in black ink.
4. Mask the image, overstamp additional stamp image(s) with VersaMark ink.

5. Let the ink dry for approximately two minutes, then color the background with blue chalk.
6. Remove mask and highlight focal image with chalks.
7. Optional: Stamp random images, stamp and cut out label, adhere to front of box with double-stick tape.
8. Fold box and secure the side with double-stick tape.

Artist Trading Card Collection Deck Boxes

Amy Wellenstein and Janet Klein

MATERIALS

Rubber Stamps: Stampotique Originals
Pigment Inkpads: VersaMark WaterMark; VersaFine Onyx Black
Dye Inkpads: Vivid!
Pastels/Chalks: Various Chalks
Papers: White Cardstock or Lightweight Posterboard
Other: Post-it Notes; Photocopy of illustration below or empty box from a deck of playing cards

INSTRUCTIONS

BOX TWO *Janet Klein*

1. Follow steps 1 and 2 in BOX ONE instructions.
2. Use direct-to-paper technique to apply inks or chalks on for background color.
3. Stamp images as desired. Fold box and secure the side with double-stick tape.

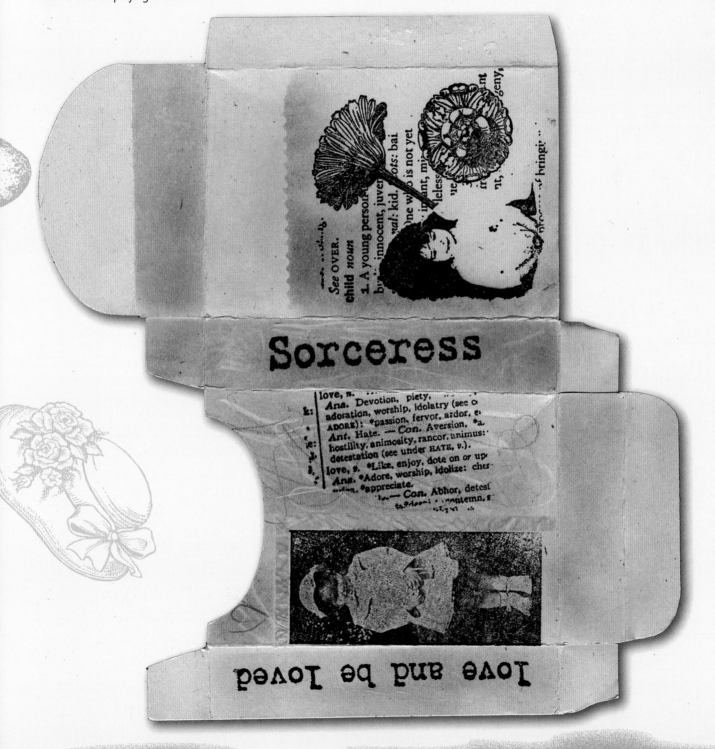

Homemade Dress

Janet Klein

MATERIALS

Rubber Stamps: Pouty Queen Figure by PaperArtsy

Dye Inkpads: Archival Jet Black

Papers: Cardstock

Paints: Yellow Twinkling H2O's; Watercolors

Colored Pencils: Prismacolor Brown, Umber, White, Flesh Tones and Soft Pink

Markers/Pens: PITT Medium Tip Artist Pen

Other: Library Pocket; Pattern Instructions; Needle; Thread; Needle Threader; Measure Tape; Buttons

Tools: Small Paintbrush; Corner Rounder; Button Hole Punch or ¹/₁₆" Punch

INSTRUCTIONS

1. Cut library pocket to ATC size; round corners and punch new corner.
2. Stamp image with black ink. Color image with colored pencil and watercolors. Enhance crown with yellow Twinkling H2O's.
3. Punch holes along left side to accommodate three buttons. Sew on buttons.
4. Use PITT pen to create faux stitches for a border.
5. Assemble needles, tape and pattern piece to inside of pocket. Glue in place.
6. Reinforce backing with cardstock cut to size (glue to library pocket).
7. Adhere tin threader in place.

Sky Blue Pink

Janet Klein

MATERIALS

Rubber Stamps: Paperbag Studios

Dye Inkpads: Archival Jet Black

Paints: Watercolors

Colored Pencils: Prismacolor Pink, Blues, Violets, White and Yellow

Markers/Pens: PITT Artist Pen

Other: Page Pebble by Making Memories

Tools: Corner Rounder, Paintbrush

INSTRUCTIONS

1. Adhere notebook paper vertically. Scribble violet and blue pastels horizontally, blend with water. Let dry. Accent with white.
2. Stamp image, color with pencils. Smear to create a transparency effect.
3. Watercolor the background violet.
4. Type word "pink", adhere under page pebble.
5. Round corners, add scrap paper.
6. Scribble white pencil around border, touch up with PITT pen.

Colored Pencils: Prismacolor Burnt Umber, Powder Blue, Jade Green, Pale Sage, Lavender and White

Other: Small Watercolor Brush; Post-it Note

Tools: Ruler

INSTRUCTIONS

1. Stamp image with black ink onto cardstock, and on a Post-it. Trim off left side of image on the Post-it for a mask.
2. Stamp again on scrap of scrapbook paper, trim, adhere, and paint shirt and dress with watercolors.
3. Color left panel with pencils, matching the hues from the paper.
4. Stamp postmark image with coffee ink on left side with mask in place. Allow to dry.
5. Color flesh tones on face.
6. Use ruler to create a border with burnt umber pencil.

Lost In Thought

Janet Klein

MATERIALS

Rubber Stamps: Woman Image by PaperArtsy; Script by Stampotique Originals

Dye Inkpads: Archival Jet Black; Ancient Page Sandalwood

Papers: Cardstock

Paints: Watercolors

Pastels/Chalks: Various Chalks

Colored Pencils: Prismacolor Yellow Ochre

Markers/Pens: PITT Medium Tip Artist Pen; Uni-ball Impact Gold Gel Pen

Tools: Ruler; Watercolor Brush

INSTRUCTIONS

1. Stamp image with sandalwood onto ochre cardstock.
2. Color face with chalks.
3. Color bodice and accent border with yellow ochre pencil.
4. Mix green and rust watercolors, paint random stripes around the card and behind image.
5. Darken hair and facial features with tip of brush.
6. Mask card while stamping script onto the large stripes.
7. Darken outside border of image with PITT pen.

Green Jellies & Pink Socks

Janet Klein

MATERIALS

Rubber Stamps: The Journey is the Destination by Paperbag Studios

Dye Inkpads: Archival Jet Black

Papers: Scenic Route; Cardstock

Paints: Watercolors; Blue, Green and Violet Twinkling H2O's

Pastels/Chalks: White and Black Neoart Wax Pastels by Caran d'Ache

Colored Pencils: Prismacolor Flesh Tones and Violets

Markers/Pens: PITT Artist Pen

INSTRUCTIONS

1. Stamp image on cardstock.
2. Use pencils to color legs with flesh tones, highlight with white, add violet in shadows.
3. Color grass with wax pastels, add Twinkling H2O's.
4. Add violet shades in shadows, paint over with Twinkling H2O's.
5. Paint shoes and socks with watercolors, accent with pencil.
6. Glue patterned paper above and below image; scribble with Neoart pastels. Add typed message.

Forest Passage on Stampboard

Anna Marie Inman

MATERIALS

Rubber Stamps: Stampscapes

Pigment Inkpads: Brilliance Cosmic Copper

Dye Inkpads: Marvy Matchables Black; Adirondack Cabin Fever; Rainbow Inkpad

Papers: Cardstock

Pens/Markers: Krylon Copper Leafing pen

Other: 3" x 3" Stampboard Tile; Krylon Crystal Clear Spray

Tools: Brayer; Scratch Tool

INSTRUCTIONS

1. Ink brayer on rainbow pad. Roll brayer back and forth over stampboard tile. Let dry completely.
2. Stamp image on tile with black ink. Let dry completely.
3. Use scratch tool to define tops of rocks and some tree limbs. Wipe away residue with tissue.
4. Edge tile with copper leafing pen.
5. Spray tile with clear acrylic aerosol.
6. Stamp image on bottom of cardstock panel in copper ink.
7. Affix tile to top of panel with double-stick tape. Mount panel onto ATC-sized cardstock.

Man

Janet Klein

MATERIALS

Rubber Stamps: Man Image by Paper Artsy

Dye Inkpads: Archival Jet Black

Papers: Cardstock, Book Page

Colored Pencils: Prismacolor Rouge, Indigo, Lavender, Flesh Tone, Chartreuse, Verte Pale and White

Markers/Pens: Green and White Jelly Roll; Aqua Soufflé by Sakura

Other: Sticker by K&Company

INSTRUCTIONS

1. Stamp man image on cardstock, stamp again on book page. Cut upper left section; trim, adhere.
2. Color flesh tones on face. Use indigo pencil in shadows and along border. Use lavender and pink in lighter shadowed areas. Accent with aqua.
3. Color border with palette provided. Scribble layers of Prismacolor on right upper corner. Scribble a false script with green and white pens. Use Soufflé pen to highlight man.
4. Place sticker in bottom corner, highlight.

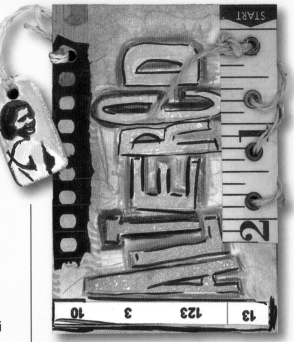

Fabulous!

Carlene Federer

MATERIALS

Rubber Stamps: PaperArtsy

Pigment Inkpads: StazOn Jet Black

Papers: Patterned Papers by Jenni Bowlin for L'il Davis Designs

Other: Image by ARTchix Studio; "Fabulous!" Word by Heidi Swapp; Ribbon

Tools: Stapler

INSTRUCTIONS

1. Adhere paper to ATC.
2. Stamp with black ink, adhere image.
3. Staple on ribbon and word "Fabulous!" to finish.

Altered ATC

Janet Klein

MATERIALS

Rubber Stamps: Altered, Script and Beauties Stamp by Stampotique Originals

Pigment Inkpads: Brilliance Peacock

Dye Inkpads: Archival Jet Black; Ancient Page Flamingo

Papers: White ATC Card; Scrap for Mini Tag; Decorative Paper

Pastels/Chalks: Various Chalks

Colored Pencils: Prismacolor Lavender, Rouge Quadrichromie, Indigo, Chartreuse, Aquamarine and Flesh Tones

Markers/Pens: PITT Brush Point Artist Pen

Other: Event Ticket; Tape Measure; Twine; Eyelets; Scrap of Black Spiral Pad Paper

Tools: Eyelet Setter, 1/8" Hole Punch; Cosmetic Sponge

INSTRUCTIONS

1. Stamp portion of Beauties image on small cardstock scrap, cut to create a tag.
2. Use pencils to color around letters, layering and altering colors.
3. Use cosmetic sponge to spread bright colored chalks around "Altered", blend well.
4. Use Flamingo ink to stamp portion of script above "Altered."
5. Glue decorative scrap in upper right corner; overlap with black spiral paper scrap. Glue portion of tape measure in bottom right corner, and ticket scrap along left edge.
6. Punch four holes along tape measure. Set eyelets and string natural colored twine or blackened waxed thread through the openings.
7. Punch one hole at top of card to hang small tag.
8. Use brush point PITT pen to accent letters with a loose, broken line.

To
drea

MATERIALS

Rubber Stamps: Script Pear, and Small Circle by Paperbag Studios

Dye Inkpads: VersaFine Onyx Black; Memories Mango

Papers: Mustard Drip by NRN Designs; Brompton by 7gypsies

Other: Metal Art Bubble Word by K&Company; Checkered Ribbon

INSTRUCTIONS

1. Cover a playing card with scrapbook paper and trim to size.
2. Use mango ink to stamp small circle on background of card.
3. Use black ink to stamp "995" on background of card.
4. Use black ink to stamp Script Pear onto paper; cut out and glue to card front.
5. Glue ribbon to card and secure metal bubble word to edge of ribbon.

Mama's Little Doll
Janet Klein

MATERIALS

Dye Inkpads: Archival Jet Black

Papers: Button Paper by K&Company; White Cardstock; Newspaper Clipping; Portions of Dress Pattern and Script Paper

Rubber Stamps: Girl by Paper Artsy; Woman Background by Stampotique Originals; Doll by Stamp in the Hand

Colored Pencils: Prismacolor Pink Tones, Soft Pink and Graphite

Pastels/Chalks: Pink and Yellow Neoart Wax Pastels by Caran d'Ache

Markers/Pens: PITT Medium Tip Artist Pen

Paints: Yellow Twinkling H2O's; Green and White Acrylic Paint

Tools: Bone Folder; Small Flat Paintbrush; Corner Rounder

INSTRUCTIONS

1. Cut white cardstock to ATC size. Whitewash a piece of newspaper with white acrylic. Let dry; glue to card. Smooth with bone folder.
2. Stamp woman on text portion of dress pattern. Adhere to card.
3. Stamp girl and doll images on white cardstock scrap. Paint as shown and cut out. Glue girl, hat, doll and cut out buttons from paper.
4. Scribble yellow Neoart pastel behind girl, use pink on edges.
5. Add green acrylic to edge of card. Use PITT pen to create faux stitches. Write "mama's little doll" with childish script; scribble graphite pencil.

Dream Fairy
Cris Cunningham

MATERIALS

Rubber Stamps: Pixie Affirmations and Alphabets by PSX; Ornate Medallions by All Night Media/Plaid; Dotted Wings by Stampers Anonymous

Dye Inkpads: Tea Dye and Faded Jeans Distress Inks; Archival Jet Black

Papers: Cardstock

Markers/Pens: Copper Leafing Pen by Krylon

Other: Girl Image by PaperWhimsy; Judikins Diamond Glaze; Rhinestones

Tools: Sponge

INSTRUCTIONS

1. Stamp Ornate Medallions background on cardstock with Tea Dye ink.
2. Stamp wings, cut out and adhere to girl image, adhere image to card.
3. Stamp phrase and cut out. Distress edges and adhere.
4. Cut out crown, add rhinestones.
5. Edge with leafing pen.

PRINCE OF FLOWERS
Sue Roddis

MATERIALS

Rubber Stamps: The Little Prince from Tim Holtz Collection and Agapanthus Cluster, both from Stampers Anonymous

Dye Inkpads: Scattered Straw, Broken China, Mustard Seed, Worn Lipstick and Dusty Concord Distress Inks; Memories Black

Papers: White Semi-Gloss Cardstock; Black Cardstock

Other: Black Thread; Eyes (from Hook and Eye Packet); JudiKins Diamond Glaze; Canvas Sheet; Canvas Pad; Gems

Tools: Small Applicator Sponges; Needle; Heat Tool

INSTRUCTIONS

1. Color a piece of canvas sheet using the worn lipstick and dusty concord Distress ink pads. Rub the pads directly onto the canvas. Wet a small sponge and use it to spread and blend the colors. Dry with a heat tool.
2. Cut a piece of the colored canvas a little smaller than ATC size. Stamp the Agapanthus cluster image to one side using the Dusty Concord ink.
3. On a piece of white cardstock stamp the Little Prince image in black. Dry and color the image using sponges and the Distress inkpads, blend and mix the colors. Attach to canvas.
4. Stitch a row of eyes along the bottom of the canvas; glue on gems.
5. Layer to black cardstock and trim to ATC size.

Not in Control
Paula Agnew Koza

MATERIALS
Rubber Stamps: Avant Garde by Stamp in the Hand

Dye Inkpads: Vivid! Black

Pastels/Chalks: Various Chalks

Markers/Pens: Red Brush Pen

Other: Yarn; Hole Reinforcement from Tag

Tools: Stipple Brush, Paper Piercer

INSTRUCTIONS
1. Stamp figure; stipple with chalk.
2. Piece holes and sew yarn following stamped lines and pierced holes.
3. Glue half of hole reinforcement as collar.
4. Use marker to edge and color hat.
5. Cut heart from red paper and adhere.

Cherish the Moment
Cris Cunningham

MATERIALS
Rubber Stamps: Pixie Sentiments by PSX; Etched Rose by Rubber Stampede; Paris Stamp Set by Cavallini & Co.; Medium Leaf Swirl by Postmodern Design

Dye Inkpads: Tattered Rose Distress Inks; Archival Sepia; Archival Jet Black

Papers: Cardstock

Markers/Pens: Copper Leafing Pen by Krylon

Other: Woman Image

Tools: Sponge

INSTRUCTIONS
1. Stamp rose background onto cardstock.
2. Adhere female image. Stamp swirl over top of card. Tear and adhere patterned paper.
3. Stamp Paris postage, cut out, distress and adhere. Stamp "cherish the moment" and adhere.
4. Distress edges with ink, edge card with leafing pen.

Stiletto
Janet Klein

MATERIALS
Rubber Stamps: Stiletto and Torn Edge by Stampotique

Dye Inkpads: Archival Jet Black

Papers: Book Page

Paints: White Acrylic

Pastels/Chalks: Portfolio Series Water Soluble Oil Pastels

Colored Pencils: Prismacolor Graphite, Blue, Pink and Black

Tools: Paintbrush

INSTRUCTIONS
1. Adhere book paper to ATC. Scribble pastels around edges, blend with a damp paintbrush.
2. Scribble lime and pink Portfolio pastel around edge of card. Blend with damp paintbrush.
3. Scribble graphite pencil over background for texture.
4. Stamp torn edge image, stamp stiletto.
5. Paint a square around the shoe image.
6. Create border with black Prismacolor around square. Accent with pink and blue. Edge card with black pencil.

Sassy
Kelly Lunceford

MATERIALS

Rubber Stamps: Express It by Making Memories; Dress Form and Boxes by Inkadinkado
Dye Inkpads: Inkstone by Rubber Stampede
Pigment Inkpads: VersaMagic Pixie Dust
Papers: Pink and Black Cardstock
Other: Blossom by Making Memories; Metal Hanger by The Card Connection; Ribbon; Pin; Clock Button; Brad; Pin; Beads
Tools: Sewing Machine

INSTRUCTIONS

1. Cut pink cardstock to ATC size, layer with black cardstock.
2. Stamp box image, sew a zigzag stitch on ATC.
3. Stamp dress form image, cut out. Tie ribbon, adhere image with pop dots, add pin to ribbon.
4. Attach metal hanger with a glue dot. Adhere clock button with glue dot; attach blossom with brad.
5. Stamp word "sassy", attach with glue dot.
6. Add beads to pin, add pin to ribbon.

Cherish Family
Kelly Lunceford

MATERIALS

Rubber Stamps: Express It by Making Memories; Cherish by BasicGrey
Dye Inkpads: StazOn Timber Brown
Papers: Marcella by K&Company; Cardstock
Other: Blossom and "Family" Brad by Making Memories; Sticker from Clearly Yours by K&Company; Picture from Children's Book; Polka Dot Ribbon by American Crafts
Tools: Sewing Machine

INSTRUCTIONS

1. Cut patterned paper and layer on ATC-sized cardstock. Sew around edges.
2. Cut out drawing from children's book and attach. Stamp word "togetherness".
3. Stamp word "cherish", cut out. Add "family" brad, attach to card with pop dots.
4. Attach bloom and brad. Add letter sticker. Knot ribbon and attach with glue dot.

Love
Kelly Lunceford

MATERIALS

Rubber Stamps: Paris Stamp by Hero Arts; Love Stamp by Anna Griffin
Dye Inkpads: Black Inkstone by Rubber Stampede; VersaMark WaterMark
Papers: Marcella by K&Company; Cardstock
Other: Shoe Charm; Ribbons
Tools: Stapler; Paintbrush

INSTRUCTIONS

1. Adhere patterned paper to cardstock as shown. Stamp image, adhere.
2. Tie ribbon around stamped image as shown.
3. Make side tab and staple to edge, stamp word "love".
4. Attach stamped image to card with mini pop dots.
5. Stamp image again onto polka dot paper, cut out circle and attach to card with pop dots.
6. Adhere shoe charm

Imagine
Kelly Lunceford

MATERIALS

Rubber Stamps: Anna Griffin
Dye Inkpads: Black by Rubber Stampede
Pigment Inkpads: Coffee Bean by Rubber Stampede; VersaMagic Tea Leaves
Papers: Cardstock
Pastels/Chalks: Various Chalks
Other: Scrabble Letters by The Card Connection; Bookplate by Making Memories; Ribbon
Tools: Blender Pen

INSTRUCTIONS

1. Layer white cardstock over green cardstock, stamp diamond image.
2. Stamp bee image as shown, then stamp onto white cardstock, cut out. Chalk wings, attach with a pop dot.
3. Adhere Scrabble letters.
4. Stamp beehive image. Color in the image, blend with blender pen.
5. Attach bookplate over beehive image with ribbon as shown.

Isle de Pelicos

Kelly Lunceford

MATERIALS

Rubber Stamps: The Isle of Pelicos Stamp Set by Nick Bantock from Limited Edition

Pigment Inkpads: ColorBox Paintbox Precious Metals; VersaMagic Tea Leaves

Dye Inkpads: StazOn Timber Brown and Olive Green; VersaMark WaterMark

Papers: Cardstock

Pencils: Watercolor Pencils

Other: Walnut Color Wash by 7gypsies, Sea Mist Pearl Embossing Powder by Stampendous; Foam Square by Making Memories; Decorative Brad by Making Memories; Word Brad by Studio K from K&Company; "Travel" Ribbon Words by Making Memories

Tools: Watercolor Brush; Heat Tool; 1/16" Hole Punch; Stapler

INSTRUCTIONS

1. Cut brown cardstock to ATC size; cut neutral cardstock slightly smaller.
2. Stamp "PELICOS". Stamp compass image, punch hole and attach decorative brad to compass.
3. Shade slightly with watercolor pencils and brush with water to blend.
4. Apply color wash randomly across card to age.
5. Set the color wash bottle onto the upper right corner in the color wash to create rings.
6. Distress the ribbon word with metallic ink and attach to upper right corner with scotch tape in the back.
7. Stamp "mail" onto cardstock, fold over edge and staple to card.
8. Stamp animal image and color.

Transparent Lady

Judith Godwin

MATERIALS

Rubber Stamps: Lady Profile by Rubber Moon; Whispers by Renaissance Art Stamps

Dye Inkpads: Archival Jet Black

Papers: Cardstock

Other: Brads; Transparency; Alcohol Inks; Blending Solution

Tools: 1/16" Hole Punch

INSTRUCTIONS

1. Stamp image on white cardstock.
2. Copy onto transparency film.
3. Mix paint, alcohol ink and blending solution on glossy white cardstock.
4. Tilt card back and forth to move solution until it covers entire area. When dry, stamp word whispers.
5. Cut cardstock to size and attach the transparency with brads.

Fragile Temperament

Amy Wellenstein

MATERIALS

Rubber Stamps: Temptress by Acey Deucy; Numeric Background by Rubbermoon; Fragile Temperament by Limited Edition

Pigment Inkpads: VersaMark WaterMark; and VersaFine Onyx Black

Papers: White Cardstock

Pastels/Chalks: Pink Chalk

Other: Post-it Notes

INSTRUCTIONS

1. Stamp Temptress on white cardstock using Onyx Black ink.
2. Mask the image and overstamp with numeric background using VersaMark ink.
3. Let the ink dry for about two minutes, then color the background with pink chalk.
4. Stamp "Fragile Temperament" across the top using Onyx Black ink.

Cute as a Button

Wendy Sullivan

MATERIALS

Rubber Stamps: Faces by Stampington & Company; Phrase, Stitches and Rickrack by Hero Arts; Buttons by All Night Media/Plaid

Pigment Inkpads: VersaMagic Night Sky

Dye Inkpads: Archival Coffee; Brilliance Black

Papers: Cardstock

Other: Shrinkable Plastic by Shrinky Dinks; Cotton Twill Tape; Foam Tape; Gel Medium

Tools: Sewing Machine; Pinking Shears; Embossing Gun; 1" Circle Punch

INSTRUCTIONS

1. Stamp Faces in black and buttons in navy ink onto shrinkable plastic.
2. Punch faces out with 1" punch.
3. Cut out buttons individually.
4. Follow instructions on package to "shrink".
5. Stamp, sew and pink paper for background.
6. Attach with gel medium.

Cheap Shoes

Judith Godwin

MATERIALS

Rubber Stamps: High Tops in a Box by Postmodern Design; Cheap Shoes by Ann-ticipations

Dye Inkpads: Archival Jet Black

Papers: Pink and White Cardstock

Paints: Watercolors

Markers/Pens: Light Brown Marker

Other: Foam Tape; Twill Tape

Tools: Paintbrush

INSTRUCTIONS

1. Distress shoes as shown using watercolors and paintbrush.
2. Stamp twill tape; adhere to shoes, trim to fit. Attach to card with foam tape.

Numbers Guy

Janet Klein

MATERIALS

Rubber Stamps: Man in Numbers Image by PaperArtsy; "1" Stamp (source unknown)

Dye Inkpads: Archival Jet Black

Papers: White Cardstock

Colored Pencils: Prismacolor Rouge, Indigo, Lavender, Flesh Tone, Chartreuse, Verte Pale, White, Orange and Yellow

Markers/Pens: Aqua and Lime Souffle by Sakura of America

Other: Life's Journey "2" Sticker by K&Company; Small Tag; Pink Eyelet

Tools: Eyelet Setter

INSTRUCTIONS

1. Stamp image with black ink on cardstock. Allow to dry.
2. Stamp "1" on small tag. Color randomly with pencils.
3. Color flesh tones on face; lavender for shadows. Color larger numbers with Souffle gel pens.
4. Color border with chartreuse pencil; layer with aqua. Add orange by shoulder line; layer with yellow.
5. Place "2" sticker above man's shoulder. Highlight with white pencil.
6. Set eyelet and thread mini tag in upper left corner.

Lyra
Ginny Carter Smallenburg

MATERIALS
Rubber Stamps: Dutch Birth Certificate by Stampers Anonymous

Dye Inkpads: Memories Black and Taupe

Other: Gel Medium; Image; Cigar Band; Tissue

Tools: Paintbrush, Circle Punch

INSTRUCTIONS
1. Crumple tissue, smooth out and wipe taupe ink over ridges.
2. Adhere tissue to card by brushing gel medium on back of card, add more gel medium over tissue.
3. Adhere image to card.
4. Stamp certificate image on vellum, punch out with circle punch, cut in half and attach. Attach cigar band.

Vision
Ginny Carter Smallenburg

MATERIALS
Rubber Stamps: Art Definition and Artful Eye by Stampers Anonymous

Dye Inkpads: Memories Black; ColorBox Bisque and Roan Chestnut

Papers: Patterned Paper by Paper Source

Other: Vintage Lens; Brass Tag by Stampers Anonymous; Brads; Clock Sticker by Sandylion Sticker Designs

INSTRUCTIONS
1. Swipe Bisque ink on backing paper, stamp definition image.
2. Ink edges with Roan Chestnut ink, add clock sticker.
3. Stamp eye image on paper and adhere to back of lens using clear tape.
4. Wrap paper scraps around card and tape down; adhere lens to center of clock sticker. Add brass tags using brads.

Fly
Ginny Carter Smallenburg

MATERIALS
Rubber Stamps: Harlequin Scrap, Abel Cash and Flying Bug Edge by Stampers Anonymous

Dye Inkpads: StazOn Jet Black, Mustard, Azure Blue and Blazing Red

Papers: Black and White Cardstock

Markers: PITT Artist Pens; White and Gold Galaxy Markers by American Craft

Tools: Small Sponges

INSTRUCTIONS
1. Cut black cardstock ATC size, cut white cardstock slightly smaller.
2. Sponge colors of ink for background on white cardstock.
3. Color image as shown with PITT pens.
4. Add hints of gold to squares on harlequin image and butterfly wings.
5. For white under wings, brush with white then gold Galaxy markers; blend as shown.

Sea Legs
Ginny Carter Smallenburg

MATERIALS
Rubber Stamps: Sea Legs by Stampers Anonymous

Dye Inkpads: Memories Black

Papers: Li'l Davis Designs

Colored Pencils: Prismacolor Pencils

Markers/Pens: PITT Artist Pens

Other: Ruler Fragment; Cord; Embellishment

INSTRUCTIONS
1. Stamp image on patterned paper, color with pencils.
2. Add ruler fragment.
3. Trim and adhere to cardstock base, add cording and embellishment.

Man on the Moon
Ginner Carter Smallenburg

MATERIALS
Rubber Stamps: Man on the Moon, Binding Edge and Moonlight by Stampers Anonymous

Dye Inkpads: Memories Black; Vivid! Straw and Taupe

Papers: Cardstock

Pastel/Chalks: Neoart Wax Pastels by Caran d'Ache

Colored Pencils: Prismacolor Pencils, Wax Pencils

Markers/Pens: PITT Artist Pens

Other: Gaffers Tape by 7gypsies

INSTRUCTIONS
1. Cover entire surface of ATC with Straw ink.
2. Stamp word image in Taupe.
3. Stamp Man in the Moon and binding edge image, color with pencils and markers as shown.
4. Trim and adhere to card, add number.

Artist Trading Cards
I'll show you mine if you show me yours!

Vintage Fairies

Carolyn Peeler

MATERIALS

Rubber Stamps: Life is a Picture and Scroll by Limited Edition; Snowflakes by PSX

Dye Inkpads: Adirondack Pesto and Latte; ColorBox Frost

Papers: Melissa Frances; Creative Imaginations

Pastels/Chalks: Red or Pink Chalk

Other: Flower; Bookplate by Making Memories; Buttons; Vintage Photographs and Images,

INSTRUCTIONS

1. Layer patterned papers, ink edges. Stamp scroll as shown.
2. Cut girls out from vintage photograph, color cheeks with chalk, adhere.
3. Stamp phrases. Assembel and add embellishments.

Chess Queen and King

Ginny Carter Smallenburg

MATERIALS

Rubber Stamps: Chess Queen and King, Harlequin Scrap and Caution Artist at Play by Stampers Anonymous

Dye Inkpads: Memories Black and Cherry Red

Papers: Cardstock; Patterned paper by FoofaLa

INSTRUCTIONS

1. Adhere patterned paper to cardstock.
2. Stamp Harlequin and Chess Queen images on patterned paper.
3. Ink the "Play" section of the Caution image, stamp on patterned paper.

Fairy Princess

Amy Wellington

MATERIALS

Rubber Stamps: Description and Label by Stampotique Originals; Fairy by Zettiology; Fairy Princess by Postmodern Design; Frame

Pigment Inkpads: VersaFine Onyx Black

Dye Inkpads: Archival Carnation

Papers: American Crafts; Cardstock

Other: Rhinestone; Foam Tape

Tools: XACTO Knife

INSTRUCTIONS

1. Stamp fairy, mask image and overstamp with description.
2. Stamp frame on patterned paper, cut out window. Layer panels using foam tape.
3. Stamp label, stamp words in label, trim and adhere. Add rhinestone.

I Will Not Sass

Jill Haglund

MATERIALS

Rubber Stamps: Three Boys by Catslife Press

Pigment Inkpads: VersaFine Onyx Black

Papers: Ivory Cardstock; I Will Not Sass by Rusty Pickle

Colored Pencils: Various Colors

Other: Metal "s" by K&Company; Playing Cards

INSTRUCTIONS

1. Glue paper to playing card.
2. Stamp image with black ink onto white card stock and cut out; adhere to ATC.
3. Color as desired (optional), add letter "s".

The New 40

Janet Klein

MATERIALS

Rubber Stamps: Woman Image by PaperArtsy; Alpha Diamonds by Catslife Press

Dye Inkpads: Archival Jet Black

Papers: Cardstock; Kraft Paper; Script Paper

Paints: Twinkling H2O's; Watercolors

Pastels/Chalks: Fuchsia Chalk

Colored Pencils: Gold Metallic Pencil by Lyra; Prismacolor White and Yellow; Watercolor Pencils

Tools: Corner Rounder; Toothbrush; Paintbrush; Cosmetic Sponge

INSTRUCTIONS

1. Dab damp toothbrush in orange watercolor paint and hold over cardstocck, pull back bristles to spatter on card surface.
2. Stamp woman image on card. Stamp alpha diamonds on craft paper, trim and cut in half.
3. Color left side of woman image with orange watercolor pencil. Feather in with yellow pencil, use moistened paintbrush to blend colors. Paint ATC as shown with watercolors and Twinkling H2O's.
4. Stain script paper with fuchsia chalk. Tear and glue to bottom of card.
5. Glue diamond border on left of card. Accent letters with yellow pencil.
6. Round corners, apply gold pencil to edges. Accent highlights with white pencil.

Likeable
Roben-Marie Smith

MATERIALS

Rubber Stamps: Grunge Alpha by Paperbag Studios

Dye Inkpads: VersaFine Onyx Black

Papers: BasicGrey; Li'l Davis Designs

Other: Button; Nail Head; Black Washer; Snap; Brad; Eyelet

Tools: Eyelet Setter; 1/16" Hole Punch

INSTRUCTIONS

1. Stamp Grunge Alpha, tear "likeable" definition from patterned paper, adhere to card.
2. Punch holes in side of card and attach washer with mini brad, snap and eyelet.
3. Attach nail head and button with glue dots.

Nothing to Wear
Wendy Sullivan

MATERIALS

Rubber Stamps: Kewpie Girl by Catslife Press; Ribbons by Hero Arts; Playtime by Rubbermoon

Pigment Inkpads: Brilliance Orchid

Dye Inkpads: Adirondack Denim and Lettuce

Paper: Cardstock; Text Weight Paper

Colored Pencils: Yellow, Blue, Black and Pink

Markers/Pens: Red, Black and Green

Tools: Stapler; Paper Crimper

INSTRUCTIONS

1. Layer cardstocks as shown, stamp with ribbon stamp.
2. Stamp words on a strip and crimp; cut to fit, staple.
3. Stamp Kewpie on text weight paper, color with pencils, distress edges, adhere.
4. Lay text weight paper over the Kewpie image. Hand draw clothing items, color as desired and tuck in pocket.

At the Chalkboard
Judith Godwin

MATERIALS

Rubber Stamps: Floor and Kid Sayings by River City Rubberworks; Betsy by B Line Designs

Pigment Inkpads: ColorBox Frost White

Papers: Cardstock; Patterned Paper

Markers/Pens: Red and Yellow

Other: JudiKins Diamond Glaze; White Embossing Powder

Tools: Heat Tool

INSTRUCTIONS

1. Stamp "Betsy" on flesh tone cardstock and patterned paper. Cut out both images.
2. Stamp floor on tan cardstock. Stamp words in white and emboss.
3. Tape floor onto bottom third of chalkboard.
4. Glue all components together.

Joyful Spirit
Roben-Marie Smith

MATERIALS

Rubber Stamps: Grateful Heart and Formula by Paperbag Studios

Dye Inkpads: StazOn Jet Black; Distress Inks

Papers: Cartaceo by Daisy D's; Textbook Paper

Other: Brads

Tools: 1/16" Hole Punch; Sponge

INSTRUCTIONS

1. Stamp Grateful Heart image onto textbook paper, tear edges.
2. Stamp and cut out phrase.
3. Stamp formula image in black, distress card.
4. Adhere the image and phrase to distressed ATC.
5. Punch holes in card, add brads.

Vanessa

Roben-Marie Smith

MATERIALS

Rubber Stamps: Vanessa by Paperbag Studios

Dye Inkpads: StazOn Jet Black

Papers: Daisy D's

Colored Pencils: Watercolor Pencils

Other: Rub-On Word by Making Me Flowers by K&Company

INSTRUCTIONS

1. Adhere paper to playing card; stamp image.
2. Color image with pencils.
3. Adhere flower and butterfly.
4. Apply rub-on word.

Hen & Chicks

Wendy Sullivan

MATERIALS

Rubber Stamps: Rooster and Chicks by Anna Griffin; Chicken Wire by Great Impressions

Pigment Inkpads: VersaMagic Red Brick

Dye Inkpads: Archival Coffee

Papers: Cardstock

Other: Eyelet; Fabric

Tools: 1/8" Hole Punch

INSTRUCTIONS

1. Stamp chicken wire background, tear and adhere as shown.
2. Punch hole, set eyelet and thread torn fabric through.
3. Stamp rooster, layer, trim and sew together.
4. Stamp chicks, trim and layer onto card.
5. Adhere rooster and chicks.

Queen Bee

Judith A Godwin

MATERIALS

Rubber Stamps: Small Bees by Inkadinkado; Large Bee Girl and Words by Catslife Press

Pigment Inkpads: VersaFine Onyx Black

Papers: Patterned Paper; Black and White Cardstock; White Vellum

Markers/Pens: Red, Peach, Blue, Orange and Yellow Markers

Other: Elf Dust Glitter Paint

INSTRUCTIONS

1. Stamp words and small bees on patterned paper.
2. Stamp Bee Girl on white cardstock. Cut out face and body, discard wings. Color as shown.
3. Stamp Bee Girl in black ink on vellum, cut out wings, paint Elf Dust on wings, adhere.

Rescued from Crash
Amy Wellenstein

MATERIALS
Rubber Stamps: Wings by Paper Artsy; Parcel Post by Toad Hall/Rubber Anarchy; Rescued from CRASH by Limited Edition
Pigment Inkpads: VersaFine Onyx Black
Dye Inkpads: Adirondack Denim
Papers: BasicGrey; Cardstock

INSTRUCTIONS
1. Stamp man image on white cardstock. Stamp Parcel Post on patterned paper, cut out window.
2. Stamp "Rescued from CRASH", layer panels using foam tape.

Mona Lisa Smiles
Wendy Sullivan

MATERIALS

Rubber Stamps: Mona Lisa by JudiKins; Text by Hero Arts; Swirl by Printworks; Art by Limited Edition; Design Fragment by Stampers Anonymous; Rectangle Shadow by Hero Arts

Dye Inkpads: Archival Coffee; Andirondak Butterscotch; Vivid! Olive and Plum
Papers: Olive, Wine and Ivory Cardstock
Other: Eyelets; Beads; Wire
Tools: Punch; Pliers

INSTRUCTIONS
1. Layer cardstock as shown.
2. Stamp shadow stamps in random colors for background, then stamp over rectangles with image.
3. Form wire into coils with pliers.
4. Insert word "art" as shown.
5. Wrap wire around bottom, add beads.

Chic
Kelly Lunceford

MATERIALS
Rubber Stamps: Purse Stamp by Inkadinkado; Design by Hero Arts
Dye Inkpads: StazOn Timber Brown
Papers: Cardstock; Vintage Paper
Other: Bookplate by Making Memories; Shoe Charm and Scrabble Letters by The Card Connection; Pink Tab by Provo Craft
Tools: Eyelet Setter

INSTRUCTIONS
1. Cut small piece of patterned paper as shown, adhere to ATC with pop dots, attach tab.
2. Stamp purse image, cut out, attach to square with pop dots. Attach shoe charm and Scrabble letters.
3. Stamp word "design" on cardstock, stitch in place.
4. Set eyelets into bookplate, frame word "chic" and attach.

I'm the Queen

Carolyn Peeler

MATERIALS

Rubber Stamps: Girl Stamp by Tracy Roos; Antique Type by Hero Arts; Collage Stamp by Inkadinkado

Dye Inkpads: Sea Shells Starfish Green; Adirondack Pitch Black

Papers: Cardstock

Pastels/Chalks: Various Chalks

Other: Rhinestones

INSTRUCTIONS

1. Stamp background with green ink. Stamp girl on white cardstock, color with chalks. Cut out girl and word "queen".
2. Stamp girl again on pink cardstock, cut out crown. Adhere image, add rhinestones to bottom of crown.
3. Stamp and write words "I'm" and "the" onto cardstock, distress edges of word strips and ATC.
4. Stitch as shown.

Delicate Flower

Amy Wellenstein

MATERIALS

Rubber Stamps: Olive Rose, Carol's Flower, Floral Background, Stripes Background and Delicate Flower by Stampotique Originals

Pigment Inkpads: VersaMark WaterMark; VersaFine Onyx Black

Dye Inkpads: Adirondack Aqua and Butterscotch

Papers: Cardstock

Pastels/Chalks: Various Chalks

Other: Post-it Notes

INSTRUCTIONS

1. Stamp Olive Rose image on card, stamp again on Post-it to make a mask.
2. Cut out the mask and layer it over the image. Overstamp stripes in VersaMark WaterMark. Wait two minutes. Color with chalks.
3. Randomly stamp large flower and flower cluster. Stamp phrase "delicate flower".
4. Lift mask.

Darling

Janet Klein

MATERIALS

Rubber Stamps: Midge, Love Definition and Circle Border by Stampotique Originals; Ticket by Hero Arts

Dye Inkpads: Archival Jet Black; Ancient Page Saffron; Adirondack Coffee

Papers: Cardstock; Patterned Paper

Paints: White Acrylic

Pastels/Chalks: Ochre and White Neoart Wax Pastels by Caran d'Ache

Colored Pencils: Prismacolor Violets, White, Yellow and Ochre

Markers/Pens: PITT Artist Pen

Other: Graphite Pencil; Post-it Notes

Tools: Paintbrush

INSTRUCTIONS

1. Whitewash patterned paper with watered-down white acrylic paint.
2. Apply Ochre pastel to card. Paint over with a damp brush to create a color wash.
3. Stamp circle border in Saffron. Stamp Midge image on ATC. Stamp again on Post-it Note and cut out to create a mask.
4. Mask girl image and stamp love definition and ticket.
5. Color girl with pencils, add Ochre dots around card. Accent dots with black PITT pen. Use ochre and white pastel to create a border.
6. Glue word "darling" in place. Scribble lightly with graphite pencil.

Love Me
Roben-Marie Smith

MATERIALS
Rubber Stamps: On the Porch by Paperbag Studios
Dye Inkpads: VersaFine Onyx Black
Papers: Making Memories; 7gypsies
Paints: White Acrylic
Colored Pencils: Watercolor Pencils
Other: Brad; Flowers; Frame
Tools: Blender Pen; Paintbrush

INSTRUCTIONS
1. Adhere patterned paper to card.
2. Dry brush frame with white acrylic.
3. Stamp image on cardstock.
4. Color image with watercolor pencils; blend with blender pen. Cut out and frame.
5. Stamp "love me" on black paper, tear and adhere to ATC.
6. Secure flower with brad.

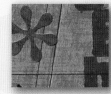

Growing
Roben-Marie Smith

MATERIALS
Rubber Stamps: Flinch 7 by Paperbag Studios
Dye Inkpads: VersaFine Onyx Black
Papers: 7gypsies; Creative Imaginations
Other: Image; Label
Tools: Dymo Label Maker

INSTRUCTIONS
1. Stamp image, layer on patterned paper as shown.
2. Tear image of child's feet, add to stamped image.
3. Add created label word to bottom of card.

Happy Day
Roben-Marie Smith

MATERIALS
Rubber Stamps: Ruled Alphabet by Paperbag Studios
Dye Inkpads: VersaFine Onyx Black
Papers: BasicGrey; 7gypsies
Other: Image by Paperbag Studios; Metal Label; Ribbon by Making Memories

INSTRUCTIONS
1. Stamp image on card, attach torn paper to edges. Tie ribbon to label, attach.
2. Adhere image to card.

To Hope
Roben-Marie Smith

MATERIALS
Rubber Stamps: To Hope by A Lost Art/Penny Black; Grunge Alpha by Paperbag Studios; Paris Postage by Tin Can Mail/Inkadinkado; Girls by All Night Media/Plaid
Dye Inkpads: VersaFine Onyx Black; Memories Port Red
Papers: Phrilly by BasicGrey; Gessato Classic Pink and Bellissimo Classic Pink by Daisy D's
Other: Playing Card
Tools: Daisy Punch by All Night Media/Plaid

INSTRUCTIONS
1. Cover a playing card with scrapbook paper and trim to size.
2. Stamp Grunge Alpha on card in red ink. Stamp Paris Postage, Girls and To Hope on card in black ink.
4. Punch daisies with paper punch and glue to card.

Happiness
Roben-Marie Smith

MATERIALS
Rubber Stamps: Best Friends by Paperbag Studios; Number 84 by Treasure Cay
Pigment Inkpads: Color Box Cat's Eye Dark Moss and Olive; Colorbok Hunter Green
Dye Inkpads: StazOn Jet Black
Papers: 7gypsies; Rusty Pickle; BasicGrey
Other: Label Maker by Dymo; Sticker by K&Company; Tab; White Gesso
Tools: Hole Punch; Eyelet Setter

INSTRUCTIONS
1. Paint one side of card with white gesso. Rub Olive and Dark Moss inks on card in that order. Add a small amount of Hunter Green.
2. Tear papers, adhere as shown. Stamp image, cut out.
3. Punch a hole in the card, attach wick tab with eyelet setter.
4. Adhere butterfly, happiness label and stamped image.

I Treasure Our Friendship

Jill Haglund

MATERIALS

Rubber Stamps: Portrait Stamp and One Man Show by Stampington and Company; Heart in Hand and Key with Star Tag by Claudine Hellmuth; I Treasure Our Friendship by Uptown Rubber Stamps; Font in Squares by Stampers Anonymous

Dye Inkpads: Archival Sepia and Denim

Papers: Cardstock; Specialty Paper

Colored Pencils: Prismacolor

Other: Metal Discs by Li'l Davis Designs

INSTRUCTIONS

1. Stamp part of One Man Show, word "dear", I Treasure Our Friendship and portrait stamp on card.
2. Stamp portrait image on corner of card. Stamp again on scrap paper and cut a mask to layer over face. Overstamp small script behind face. Lift masks.
3. Stamp portrait image again; cut out and layer on top; overstamp key image, "d" in dear and hand with heart.
4. Layer onto specialty papers as shown, adhere metal elements.

Forget Me Not

Jean Hawkins

MATERIALS

Rubber Stamps: African Boy and Country Tree by A Stamp in the Hand; Weeds and Background by Little Lace Lady; Forget Me Not by Rubbermoon; Three Indian Girls by Old Town Crafts; Mesas by Beeswax; Great Grandma Mary Catherine by River City Rubberworks; Chief by Acey Deucy

Pigment Inkpads: Various Colors ColorBox Cat's Eye Inkpads

Dye Inkpads: Memories Art Print Brown; Adirondack Butterscotch

Papers: Cardstock

Colored Pencils: Prismacolor Red and Brown

Markers/Pens: Copper by Krylon

Tools: Sponges

INSTRUCTIONS

1. Stamp images in brown ink. Stamp again on scrap paper and cut out to make masks.
2. Temporarily adhere masks overstamped images.
3. Stamp background and foreground images in brown ink.
4. Sponge ColorBox inks onto cardstock as shown. Color highlights with pencils. Edge cards with copper pen.

Green Queen

Amy Wellenstein

MATERIALS

Rubber Stamps: Electra by Stamp Camp; Pretty Paisley by Stampin' Up; Retro Wave by Printworks; Circle of Dots and Alphabet by Ephemera Design Studio

Pigment Inkpads: VersaMark WaterMark; VersaFine Onyx Black

Papers: Cardstock

Pastels/Chalks: Green Chalks

Other: Post-it Notes

Tools: Applicators

INSTRUCTIONS

1. Stamp woman image on ATC, stamp twice again to create masks; one of woman and one of entire image. Mask woman and overstamp with dots as shown.
2. Mask entire image, then overstamp with VersaMark WaterMark.
3. Using applicators, color background with green chalks. Lift mask and wait two minutes, then color image as shown.
4. Stamp wave along the bottom, then stamp letter "Q".

Tunnel Vision

Wendy Sullivan

MATERIALS

Rubber Stamps: Eye by JudiKins; Optical Box by Hero Arts; DaVinci Background by Rubber Dub Dub; Vision by Stampers Anonymous

Pigment Inkpads: Fresco Sicilian Spice; VersaMagic Mango Madness and Navy Blue

Dye Inkpads: Brilliance Black

Papers: Cardstock

Paints: Colbalt Blue and Moss Agate Twinkling H2O's

Colored Pencils: Brown, Blue and Green

Other: Slide Mount; Crystal Lacquer

Tools: Heat Tool; Stipple Brush; Small Watercolor Brush; Foam Brush

INSTRUCTIONS

1. Stamp background onto cardstock. Stipple inks and rub with inks directly to ATC.
2. Stamp eye image; apply ink to eye with paintbrush and a bit of water. Allow to dry. Apply crystal lacquer in center of eye.
3. Stamp optical box on slide mount and stipple with blue ink.
4. Mount the eye image behind the opening of the slide mount and adhere to ATC. Cut out word from "vision" stamp and adhere to card.

Tickled Pink

Wendy Sullivan

MATERIALS

Rubber Stamps: Le Bebe Jumeau by Oxford Impressions; French Bebes by ArtDreams; Tickled Pink by Rubbermoon; French Text by Non Sequitur; Girl

Dye Inkpads: Adirondack Coffee and Raisin

Papers: Cardstock

Other: Embossing Powder; Vintage Photograph; Brad

Tools: 1/16" Hole Punch; Heat Tool

INSTRUCTIONS

1. Layer cardstocks as shown. Stamp Le Bebe Jumea, Text and Bebes.
2. Attach image to card, stamp words.
3. Cover brad with Raisin ink, emboss with clear embossing powder and heat set; repeat. Punch card and attach brad.

PAMPER

Oh, So Pretty

Wendy Sullivan

MATERIALS

Rubber Stamps: Corset and Text by Oxford Impressions; Text by A Stamp in the Hand; Ribbon by Hero Arts, Lace by Rubber Stampede; Phrase by Rubbermoon

Pigment Inkpads: VersaMagic Hint of Pesto; Fresco Vatican Wine

Dye Inkpads: Whispers Starry Night

Papers: Patterned Paper by Anna Griffin; Cardstock

Other: Embossing Powder; Twill Tape; Vintage Garter Clip; Snap

Tools: Heat Tool; Eyelet Setter; Paintbrush; 1/16" Hole Punch

INSTRUCTIONS

1. Stamp ribbon on cardstock, then stamp words "Oh, so pretty" on top, cut out.
2. Stamp corset in wine and cut out, stamp background. Tear and adhere patterned paper.
3. Stamp text on twill, thread through garter. Attach garter, corset and phrase.
4. Punch hole and attach garter.
5. Adhere

Sweet is She

Wendy Sullivan

MATERIALS

Rubber Stamps: Travel Words by PSX; Optician Lens by Oxford Impressions

Pigment Inkpads: Brilliance Gold

Dye Inkpads: Archival Coffee; Brilliance Black

Papers: Cardstock

Colored Pencils: Pink and Blue

Markers/Pens: Gold Pen by Krylon

Other: Ribbons; Buckle; Mica Sheet; Gold Embossing Powder

Tools: Heat Tool; Decorative Punch; Stipple Brush

INSTRUCTIONS

1. Stamp travel words, stipple to age. Use punch on all corners of black cardstock, layer on top of travel words, layer papers as shown.
2. Stamp opticians lens, emboss with gold powder. Cut away the ribbon edge from the lens top. Stamp again, cut out face portion, age. Edge opticians lens with gold Krylon and adhere the face portion.
3. Cut a piece of mica to cover the face portion and adhere with double-stick tape.
4. Thread ribbon and buckle to opening in opticians lens and attach lens to card with foam tape.

Think Outside the Box

Amy Wellenstein

MATERIALS

Rubber Stamps: Eclectic by PaperArtsy; Head by Fishbone Graphics; Block #1 by Stamp it!

Pigment Inkpads: VersaFine Onyx Black

Papers: White and Black Cardstock; Cherry Pie and Lollipop Shoppe Paper by BasicGrey

Other: Foam Tape

INSTRUCTIONS

1. Stamp man image in black ink on white cardstock.
2. Stamp Block #1 on patterned paper; cut out window.
3. Layer panels using foam tape.
4. Stamp "THINK OUTSIDE THE BOX" on scrap of white cardstock; layer on black cardstock and adhere.

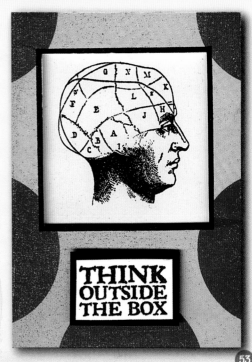

Cherish
Roben-Marie Smith

MATERIALS
Rubber Stamps: Holding Hands by Paperbag Studios
Dye Inkpads: VersaFine Onyx Black
Papers: BasicGrey; K&Company
Paints: White Acrylic
Other: Buttons
Tools: Stapler; Corner Edger; Paintbrush

INSTRUCTIONS
1. Adhere patterned paper to card, round corners.
2. Using the dry brush technique, apply white paint over paper.
3. Stamp word "cherish" on striped paper, staple and attach buttons.

Bench
Roben-Marie Smith

MATERIALS
Rubber Stamps: Simple Pleasures by Paperbag Studios
Dye Inkpads: VersaFine Onyx Black
Papers: Cardstock; FoofaLa
Other: Black Nail Head; File Tab by 7gypsies

INSTRUCTIONS
1. Adhere paper to cardstock, stamp image.
2. Adhere patterned paper to inside of tab, attach to card. Adhere nail head to end of tab with glue dots.

Through the Years
Roben-Marie Smith

MATERIALS
Rubber Stamps: Lone Tree by Paperbag Studios
Dye Inkpads: VersaFine Onyx Black Papers: Autumn Leaves
Other: Metal Word Charm by Making Memories; Buttons

INSTRUCTIONS
1. Stamp image on patterned paper, adhere to cardstock and trim.
2. Using glue dots, adhere metal word charm and buttons to card.

Keep True
Roben-Marie Smith

MATERIALS
Rubber Stamps: Keep True by Paperbag Studios
Dye Inkpads: StazOn Jet Black
Papers: Daisy D's
Colored Pencils: Blue Watercolor Pencil
Other: Ticket; Vintage Image
Tools: Blender Pen

INSTRUCTIONS
1. Stamp image on patterned paper, glue to playing card.
2. Cut out girls from photo, color bow, blend with pen. Adhere girls and ticket as shown.

Noel
Roben-Marie Smith

MATERIALS
Rubber Stamps: Lights by Paperbag Studios
Dye Inkpads: StazOn Jet Black
Papers: 7gypsies
Colored Pencils: Watercolor Pencils
Other: Metal Saying; Rub-On Words by Making Memories
Tools: Blender Pen

INSTRUCTIONS
1. Cut two sizes of papers as shown. Stamp light post on one paper, layer on red script paper.
2. Color image with watercolor pencils, blend colors with pen, adhere papers to playing card.
3. Sew around top image with zigzag stitch and gold thread.

CHERISH

through the years

It's the simple joys, the simple pleasures the heart remembers and dearly treasures.

Noël

The way to know lif

43331 Vb
C. CARD

Keep
true
to the
dreams
of your
youth.

Black Cat

Amy Wellenstein

MATERIALS

Rubber Stamps: Black Cat Mystery Plate and 2 by PaperArtsy; Number Border by Limited Edition; Suds Background by Stamp Camp

Pigment Inkpads: VersaMark WaterMark; VersaFine Onyx Black

Papers: Cardstock

Pastels/Chalks: Various Chalks

Other: Post-it Notes

INSTRUCTIONS

1. Stamp Black Cat on Post-it to create mask; cut out.
2. Stamp Black Cat on ATC, mask image and in VersaMark WaterMark for textured background. Wait two minutes and color background with chalks.
3. Stamp Number Border to finish.

Happy Valentine's Day

Amy Wellenstein

MATERIALS

Rubber Stamps: Happy Valentine's Day by Rubber Soul; All Other Images by Stampotique Originals

Pigment Inkpads: VersaMark WaterMark; VersaFine Onyx Black

Papers: Cardstock

Other: Foam Tape

INSTRUCTIONS

1. Stamp Little Girl image on ATC, stamp again to create a mask. Cut mask.
2. Mask the image and overstamp with VersaMark WaterMark. Wait two minutes.
3. With the mask still in place, color background, remove mask and color girl image.
4. Stamp Long Label and Happy Valentine's Day, trim and adhere with foam tape, then stamp doily image.

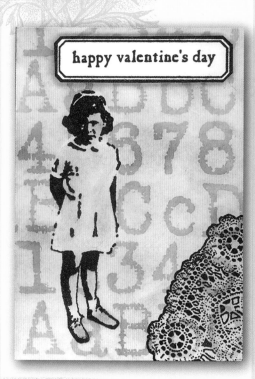

Mocha Style

Wendy Sullivan

MATERIALS

Rubber Stamps: Woman by Acey Deucy; Style is Eternal by Hero Arts; Border by Penny

Pigment Inkpads: VersaMagic Pixie Dust

Dye Inkpads: Ancient Page Chocolate

Papers: Cardstock

Other: Ribbon; Foam Tape

INSTRUCTIONS

1. Stamp background images on ATC; add ribbon.
2. Stamp woman and mat as shown.

40 Something
Jill Haglund

MATERIALS
Rubber Stamps: PaperArtsy
Pigment Inkpads: ColorBox Blue
Dye Inkpads: Memories Cherry Red
Papers: Cardstock
Other: Metal Ring by 7gypsies; Judikins Diamond Glaze
Tools: Heat Tool

INSTRUCTIONS
1. Rub ATC with blue inkpad, heat set.
2. Stamp female image and number border.
3. Adhere metal ring over number 40 and fill with Diamond Glaze.

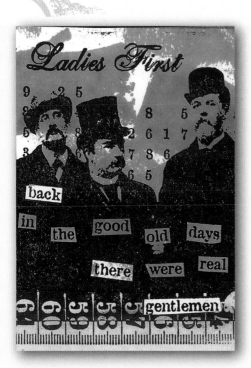

Ladies First
Jill Haglund

MATERIALS
Rubber Stamps: Ladies First Plate by PaperArtsy
Pigment Inkpads: VersaFine Onyx Black; ColorBox Yellow Citrus
Dye Inkpads: Ancient Page Light Brown
Papers: Cardstock

INSTRUCTIONS
1. Randomly press brown inkpad onto ATC, then stamp image as shown.
2. Stamp image twice on scrap paper. Color and cut out ruler, adhere to ATC.
3. On the other image cut out words and adhere to ATC.

Sweetheart
Janet Klein

MATERIALS
Rubber Stamps: Girl Image by PaperArtsy
Dye Inkpads: Archival Jet Black
Papers: Cardstock; Patterned Paper by K&Company; Book Text; Notebook Paper
Paints: White Acrylic
Pastels/Chalks: Olive, Rust and White Neoart Wax Pastels by Caran d'Ache
Colored Pencils: Prismacolor
Other: Photo Corners; Dress Pattern

INSTRUCTIONS
1. Whitewash book page with watered down acrylic paint. Trim desired portion of page, glue to card.
2. Apply olive and white pastel to card, paint over with a damp brush to create a color wash.
3. Stamp girl image, color, cut out and adhere.
4. Glue spiral border, floral scrap, text and pattern piece to card. Adhere word "sweetheart" over text.
5. Accent with wax pastels as shown, add photo corners to finish.

Love it.

Best Friend
Amy Wellenstein

MATERIALS
Rubber Stamps: Safety Pin Border, Friend Word and Measuring Tape by Stampotique Originals; Best Friends Image and Phrase by Paperbag Studios

Pigment Inkpads: VersaMark WaterMark; VersaFine Onyx Black

Dye Inkpads: Archival Crimson

Papers: Cardstock

Pastels/Chalks: Various Chalks

Other: Post-it Note

INSTRUCTIONS
1. Stamp best friend image and phrase on card; stamp again on Post-it to make a mask.
2. Mask girls and overstamp the safety pin border several times in VersaMark WaterMark. Wait two minutes.
3. With the mask still in place, color background with chalks as shown.
4. Remove the mask and color the focal image with chalks.
5. Stamp Measuring Tape and the word "Friend".

S is for Skip; S is for Sister; S is for Shy, S is for Story
Christy Hawkins

MATERIALS
Rubber Stamps: Margaret Reading by Enchanted Ink; Jane by B Line Designs; Alphabet by Stampers Anonymous; Splatter by Treasure Cay; Girl Skipping by Stampland; Two Girls by All Night Media/Plaid

Dye Inkpads: Memories Brown and Black

Papers: Creative Imaginations; Cardstock

Pastels/Chalks: Various Chalks

Other: Matte Spray Sealer

INSTRUCTIONS
1. Cut cardstock for four ATCs. Tear strips of paper, adhere as shown.
2. Stamp splatter image, adhere to edge of the card.
3. Stamp letters to spell words for each ATC.
4. Add desired colors to letter squares with chalks, spray to seal. Cut out letters, adhere to cards.
5. Apply black ink to edges of the cards.

Carefree
Roben-Marie Smith

MATERIALS
Rubber Stamps: Always Young by Paperbag Studios

Dye Inkpads: StazOn Jet Black

Papers: BasicGrey; Provo Craft

Colored Pencils: Watercolor Pencils

Other: Rub-On Words by Making Memories; Bubble Letter by Li'l Davis Designs

Tools: Blender Pen

INSTRUCTIONS
1. Cover card with patterned paper, tear a different piece of patterned paper, adhere to side of card as shown.
2. Stamp image, cut out, adhere. Add metal element "C", use rub-ons for word "carefree".

Vintage Sewing Set

Wendy Sullivan

MATERIALS

Rubber Stamps: Dress Form, Scissors, Needle Case and Bow by Oxford Impressions; The Dressmaker Sheet and Press Button by B Line Designs; Measuring Tape and Splotches by Treasure Cay; Script by A Stamp in the Hand; Safety Pins by Club Scrap; Thread Spools by Designing Women; Rick Rack and Stitches by Hero Arts; Vintage by Treasure Cay; Forget Me Not by Rubbermoon; Grace and Truth by Leave Memories; Numbers by Oxford Impressions

Dye Inkpads: Archival Coffee and Butterscotch; Whispers Grand Cranberry; Vivid! Olive

Papers: K&Company; Cardstock

Other: Labels by Li'l Davis Designs; Buttons; Snaps; Pins; Needles; Lace; Hook and Eye Fastener; Yarn; Cardboard; String; Eyelets

Tools: Eyelet Setter; 1/8" Hole Punch

INSTRUCTIONS

1. Tear or cut patterned papers, age edges and stamp any background accents.
2. Stamp images on cardstock, cut out and age.
3. Adhere patterned papers to ATCs, then add cut out images.
4. Stamp labels with word images, adhere to cards.
5. Finish cards by adding sewing notions as shown.

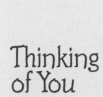

Love

Cris Cunningham

MATERIALS

Rubber Stamps: Pixie Sentiments and Alphabets by PSX; Couple by Inkadinkado

Dye Inkpads: Archival Jet Black

Papers: DieCuts With A View; Cardstock

Colored Pencils: Prismacolor

Markers/Pens: Copper Leafing Pen

Other: Female Image

INSTRUCTIONS:

1. Collage patterned papers on card.
2. Stamp Couple image, cut out, color and adhere to card.
3. Stamp words, cut out and adhere to card.
4. Edge card with leafing pen.

Thinking of You

Jill Haglund

MATERIALS

Rubber Stamps: Acey Deucey; Thinking of You by Inkadinkado; Compass by PSX; Heart

Dye Inkpads: Archival Sepia

Papers: Cardstock

Colored Pencils: Various Colors

Other: Tags; Ribbons; Beads; Fibers; Coin Envelope

INSTRUCTIONS

1. Stamp Acey Duecy image and heart on coin envelope.
2. Stamp "Thinking of You" on tag. Thread and tie beads, small round heart, stamped tag and fibers to larger tag.
3. Use colored pencils to enhance tags and envelope.
4. Slip tag in envelope. Layer onto cardstock.

Journey

Irene Eiland

MATERIALS

Rubber Stamps: Face by Magenta; Ticket by Invoke Arts; Floral Background by Sandy Miller

Pigment Inkpads: VersaMark WaterMark

Dye Inkpads: Archival Jet Black

Papers: Cardstock

Colored Pencils: Red

Other: Photo Corners

INSTRUCTIONS

1. Stamp floral background with VersaMark WaterMark.
2. Stamp face on cardstocks using black ink.
3. Cut images to make a collage as shown, color lips with red pencil.
4. Stamp ticket onto cardstock, cut out, glue on photo corner and adhere to ATC.

Paris

Cris Cunningham

MATERIALS

Rubber Stamps: Pixie Alphabets and Decorative Flourish by PSX; Paris Stamps by Cavallini & Co., Rose Background by Rubber Stampede

Dye Inkpads: Archival Sepia and Jet Black

Papers: Cardstock

Markers/Pens: Copper Leafing Pen

Other: Boy Image

INSTRUCTIONS

1. Stamp rose background on card, stamp Eiffel Tower image and cut out.
2. Cut out boy and Paris image, adhere.
3. Stamp word "Bonjour", overstamp with Flourish.
4. Age edges with sepia ink.

Deco Dance

Lisa Gifford

MATERIALS

Rubber Stamps: DANCE and Female Image (Source Unknown)

Dye Inkpads: Adirondack Aqua; Memories Midnight Blue

Papers: Cardstock

Tools: Stipple Brush

INSTRUCTIONS

1. Stamp image in aqua on glossy cardstock cut to ATC size.
2. Stamp DANCE in blue; stipple edge of ATC.

This is a Tree

Janet Klein

MATERIALS

Rubber Stamps: Script by Paperbag Studios; Three Faces by Renaissance Art Stamps

Dye Inkpads: Archival Jet Black and Library Green; Ancient Page Saffron

Papers: Cardstock

Pastels/Chalks: Various Chalks

Colored Pencils: Prismacolor Green, Flesh, Blue, Orange, Pink, Ochre and Violet

Markers/Pens: Black Gel Pen

Tools: Corner Rounder

INSTRUCTIONS

1. Stamp circle in top center of card, mask a ¼" width for trunk.
2. Stamp and scribble for trunk, accent as shown.
3. Ink faces one at a time and mask to stamp one image at a time. Stamp a face on both sides of the tree.
4. Use pen to draw child-like body shapes on faces. Write "this is a tree" in the spaces. Color in dresses and faces.
5. Use chalks and pencils to color ATC.
6. Write quotation around edge with black gel pen.

Serendipity

Pat Truitt

MATERIALS

Papers: Gold Metallic Cardstock; Mulberry Paper; Patterned Papers

Other: Excelsior Moss; Button; Purple Thread

INSTRUCTIONS

1. Tear Mulberry paper, adhere paper and moss to card.
2. Cut patterned paper into squares, adhere to gold cardstock.
3. Thread button and add to card.

Kimono

Karen Shafer

MATERIALS

Rubber Stamps: Chinese Calligraphy by All Night Media/Plaid; Chinese Postage by Tamarind

Papers: Cardstock; Patterned Papers

Pigment Inkpads: Brilliance Galaxy Gold

Dye Inkpads: StazOn Jet Black

Markers/Pens: Metallic Gold Marker

Other: Various Colors Adirondack Alcohol Inks; Image; Coin

INSTRUCTIONS

1. Make origami kimono, mount on black cardstock.
2. Make background using alcohol inks and gold marker.
3. Stamp postage over background.
4. Cut tag out of black paper, stamp with Chinese Calligraphy.
5. Attach gold coin to tag with metallic threads, edge with gold marker.

Asian Beauty

Jill Haglund

MATERIALS

Rubber Stamps: Asian Geisha by Acey Duecy; Floral Stem by PSX

Dye Inkpads: Memories Black and Cherry Red

Papers: Far and Away; Cardstock

Paints: Portfolio SeriesWater Soluble Oil Pastels

Other: Silk Flowers; Flower Brads

Tools: 1/8" Hole Punch

INSTRUCTIONS

1. Tear paper and layer to card.
2. Stamp geisha and floral stem cut out and adhere to ATC. Edge card in red ink.
3. Scribble green pastels, rub to blend. Color face and blend.
4. Punch holes and add flowers with brads.

1. Make ATC using specialty papers.
2. Make small origami crane out of chiyogami paper; adhere and add mini gyp.
3. Stamp word "fragments", tear around image, adhere as shown.
4. Tuck in gyp behind crane.

Blue Crane

Pat Truitt

MATERIALS

Rubber Stamps: Peace Crane by Hero Arts

Dye Inkpads: ColorBox Indigo

Papers: Cardstock; Patterned Paper; Chiyogami Paper

Other: Dried Flowers

INSTRUCTIONS:

1. Adhere patterned paper and chiyogami paper to front of card.
2. Stamp crane, tear around stamped image and ink edges, adhere.

Fragments

Pat Truitt

MATERIALS

Rubber Stamps: Alphabet Stamps by PSX

Dye Inkpads: ColorBox Indigo

Papers: Cardstock; Patterned Paper; Chiyogami Paper

Other: Dried Flowers

Tools: 1" Hole Punch

INSTRUCTIONS:

1. Adhere patterned papers as shown.
2. Create origami crane.
3. Punch circle from blue paper.
4. Assemble and stamp words.

Our Friendship Hits The Spot!

Pat Truitt

MATERIALS

Rubber Stamps: Cara Mia by Acey Deucy

Pigment Inkpads: ColorBox Black

Papers: Cardstock; Patterned Paper

Markers/Pens: Yellow Marker

Other: Flowers; Buttons; Mesh; Rick Rack

Tools: Circle Punch

INSTRUCTIONS

1. Adhere patterned papers to cardstock; add ribbon.
2. Stamp head with butterfly on cardstock; punch out circle as shown, color with marker.
3. Add mesh, place rubber stamped circle on top.
4. Sew on button, glue on flowers
5. Adhere rick rack.

Wild Thing

Pat Truitt

MATERIALS

Rubber Stamps: Giraffe by Mostly Animals

Dye Inkpads: StazOn Timber Brown

Paper: Cardstock

Other: Fabric; Excelsior Moss; Bead; Ribbon; Reed

INSTRUCTIONS

1. Stamp giraffe on fabric, fray edges, adhere to ATC.
2. Randomly add moss, sew on reed, ribbon and bead as shown.

Ichiyo (One Leaf)

Pat Truitt

MATERIALS

Rubber Stamps: Chinese Calligraphy by All Night Media/Plaid

Dye Inkpads: StazOn Jet Black

Papers: Cardstock; Calligraphy Paper

Other: Preserved Leaf; Excelsior Moss

Tools: Corner Rounder

INSTRUCTIONS

1. Round corners of ATC; tear calligraphy paper, adhere.
2. Stamp Chinese writing onto ivory cardstock, tear and adhere to ATC.
3. Place excelsior moss on top and adhere leaf.

By the Sea

Wendy Sullivan

MATERIALS

Rubber Stamps: Ocean View Hotel, By the Sea, Numbers, Postage Cancellation and Ticket by Oxford Impressions; Seahorse by Creative Images; Nautilus Shell by Anita's Art Stamps; Sun, Sand, Surf Words by Leave Memories

Dye Inkpads: Adirondack Coffee, Terra Cotta and Stonewash

Papers: Cardstock

Paints: Making Memories Cornflower

Other: Vintage Photo; Brad; Binder Clip; Twill Tape

Tools: 1/16" Hole Punch

CAUTION: ARTIST AT PLAY

INSTRUCTIONS:

1. Stamp Ocean View Hotel, enlarge image on a copy machine. Distress with ink; adhere to ATC.
2. Stamp "by the sea" on twill tape, adhere.
3. Paint binder clip and brad, attach as shown.
4. Stamp nautilus shell, words, postage cancellation, seahorse, ticket and numbers with coffee ink. Cut out.
5. Adhere vintage image, layer on cardstock, insert in clip. Attach clip to brad.

grinning like a fool

dressed-up-to-kill.

a silly little boy.

It was hardly wise to taunt him.

I don't dress to please you.

he stood there, tall and proud

Men In Hats

Claudine Hellmuth

MATERIALS

Rubber Stamps: Poppet Stamps by Claudine Hellmuth
Pigment Inkpads: Archival Jet Black
Papers: 140 lb. Watercolor Paper
Paints: Various Acrylics including Titan Buff by Golden
Markers/Pens: PITT Artist Pen; Various Colors Sakura Permapaque
Other: Decorative Tissue Papers; Gel Medium; Old Book
Tools: Wide Paintbrush

INSTRUCTIONS

1. Cut watercolor paper ATC size; glue decorative tissue papers to ATCs with a gel medium.
2. Photocopy pictures, cut out head portions. Draw bodies on ATCs.
3. Adhere men's heads to bodies, paint bodies, overwash with Titan Buff acrylic.
4. Stamp hats onto white paper; color using markers, cut out and adhere.
5. Outline in black; add sayings cut from old book.

mad
about
you

You say I'm "catty", like it's a bad thing.

Chill Out
Deanna Furey

MATERIALS

Rubber Stamps: Cat by JudiKins; Big Flower, Fancy Swirls, Shadow Boxes and Small Flowers by Hero Arts

Pigment Inkpads: Brilliance Black; ColorBox Pearlescent Coral, Yellow, Lime, Orange, Lavender and Orchid

Dye Inkpads: Archival Tangerine and Banana

Papers: Cardstock

Other: Sequins; Words by me and my BIG ideas; Foam Tape

INSTRUCTIONS

1. Stamp flowers and shadow boxes on ATC; mat with black.
2. Stamp and cut out cat. Adhere body to card, attach head with foam tape.
3. Adhere sequins for eyes, add sticker.
4. Apply rub-on words.

You GO girl !

I'm Catty
Deanna Furey

MATERIALS

Rubber Stamps: Plain Cat and Striped Cat by Postmodern Design; Catty Phrase by Art Impressions; Holiday Baubles by Hero Arts

Pigment Inkpads: VersaMagic Chalk Sea Breeze and Magnolia Bud; Brilliance Graphite Black

Papers: Cardstock

Other: Clear Embossing Powder; Foam Tape

INSTRUCTIONS

1. Stamp Holiday Baubles on cardstock.
2. Stamp cats, sprinkle on embossing powder, heat set. Cut out cats, glue to ATC.
3. Stamp phrase.

Chill Out

You Go Girl
Deanna Furey

MATERIALS

Rubber Stamps: Cat by JudiKins

Pigment Inkpads: Brilliance Graphite Black

Other: Marilyn Monroe Playing Cards; Google Eyes; Sticker by me & my BIG ideas

INSTRUCTIONS

1. Stamp cat, cut out head and glue to body. Adhere google eyes.
2. Cut a tail shape from black paper and glue to card, add sticker.

Groovy Cat
Deanna Furey

MATERIALS

Rubber Stamps: Cat and Ricky Ticky Stickies Flower Cube by JudiKins

Pigment Inkpads: Brilliance Graphite Black, Pearlescent Lavender, Sky Blue and Coral

Papers: Vellum; Cardstock

Other: Bead Fringe

Tools: Large Square Punch and Small Square Punch

INSTRUCTIONS

1. Stamp flower in various inks on ATC.
2. Stamp cat in Graphite Black on vellum paper.
3. Punch large square in cardstock, punch center with the smaller punch to make a frame.
4. Glue a piece of bead fringe to back of frame and attach to ATC with foam tape.

Possibilities
Jill Holmes

MATERIALS

Rubber Stamps: Possibilities by Eclectic Omnibus

Pigment Inkpads: Brilliance Graphite Black

Papers: Cardstock; Anna Griffin; EK Success

Other: Ribbon; Eyelets; Fibers; Button; String; Photograph; Photograph Marker

Tools: ⅛" Punch; Eyelet Setter

INSTRUCTIONS

1. Adhere patterned paper, photograph and punched heart to ATC.
2. Stamp Possibilities and word "love", write word "grows".
3. Punch hole; set eyelet; thread fibers and ribbon.
4. Knot string through button and adhere to ATC.

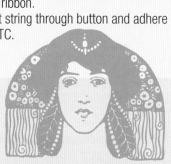

Queen for A Day
Jill Haglund

MATERIALS

Rubber Stamps: Miss May by Tracy Roos; Label by Stampotique Originals

Pigment Inkpads: ColorBox Orchid; VersaFine Onyx Black

Dye Inkpads: Memories Cherry Red

Papers: Cardstock

Pastels/Chalks: Various Chalks

Other: Aluminum Tape

Tools: Heat Tool

INSTRUCTIONS

1. Cover ATC with Orchid ink, stamp Miss May image.
2. Stamp image again, color face with chalks. Cut out and adhere to stamped image on ATC.
3. Stamp Miss May again onto aluminum tape, heat set and cut out. Adhere to card.

Casablanca
Karen Shafer

MATERIALS

Rubber Stamps: Casablanca by Stamp Francisco; Might As Well by Echoes des Voyages; Q-Bit by JudiKins

Dye Inkpads: StazOn Jet Black

Papers: Cardstock

Other: Eyelets; Handmade Tassel

Tools: ⅛" Punch; Eyelet Setter; Foam Tape

INSTRUCTIONS

1. Stamp image twice on cardstock, cut out camel from one image.
2. Make and hang tassel around camel's neck, adhere camel with foam tape.
3. Stamp saying, set eyelets, stamp corner images. Layer ont ATC sized cardstock.

Lady in Red

Jane Maley

MATERIALS

Rubber Stamps: Vixen by Endless Creations

Dye Inkpads: StazOn Jet Black

Paper: Cardstock; Patterned Paper

Colored Pencils: Prismacolor

Other: Ribbon; Gamsol Solution by Gamblin; Blending Stumps; Ruby Red Stickles by Ranger

INSTRUCTIONS

1. Stamp image, tear out; color hair and lips. Using Gamsol and blending stumps, blend colored areas.
2. Embellish woman with Ruby Red Stickles. Adhere image to red cardstock; add ribbon.

Olivia

Michi Michaelson

MATERIALS

Rubber Stamps: Shakespeare Heroines by The Stampsmith

Dye Inkpads: Archival Aqua

Papers: Cardstock; Glossy Cardstock

Other: Dried Flowers

Tools: Diecut Machine; Texture Plate

INSTRUCTIONS

1. Using texture plate, dry emboss cardstock. Stamp image on glossy cardstock and cut out, adhere.
2. Add dried flowers.

Queen of Her World

Jane Maley

MATERIALS

Rubber Stamps: Queen of Her World by The Queen's Dresser Drawers

Dye Inkpads: StazOn Cactus Green, Cherry Pink, Sunflower Yellow and Jet Black

Papers: Cardstock

Other: Rhinestones; Glitter; Stickers by Making Memories

Tools: Cosmetic Sponges.

INSTRUCTIONS

1. Randomly apply inkpad directly to paper with sponge to create colored background. Use circular motions to blend colors together, stamp image.
2. Add rhinestones and glitter to crown, add title with stickers.

Einstein

Karen Shafer

MATERIALS

Rubber Stamps: Imagine by Stampers Anonymous

Dye Inkpads: StazOn Jet Black

Papers: Cardstock

Colored Pencils: Various Colors

Markers/Pens: Metallic Gold Marker

Other: Hair from Sheepskin Rug; Photocopy of Einstein

Tools: Xacto Knife

INSTRUCTIONS

1. Cut two sides of card stock and edge in gold as show.
2. Adhere photocopy of Einstein to top cardstock.
3. Stamp word "imagine", color and adhere under photo.
4. Use Xacto knife to cut around scalp and insert pieces of "hair", tape to back.
5. Stamp "E=MC2".

Fleur Girl

Janet Klein

MATERIALS

Rubber Stamps: Fleur Girl by Stampotique Originals

Pigment Inkpads: VersaMark WaterMark

Dye Inkpads: Archival Black

Papers: Cardstock; KI Memories

Paints: Watercolors

Pastels/Chalks: Various Chalks

Colored Pencils: Prismacolor

Markers/Pens: PITT Artist Pen

Tools: Corner Rounder; Cosmetic Sponge; Heat Tool; Small Tip Water Brush by Ninji

INSTRUCTIONS

1. Stamp Fleur Girl image, stamp again to create a mask. Cut out. Keep both positive and negative of mask.
2. Paint desired areas using watercolors.
3. Mask focal image, stamp background image. Stamp with VersaMark WaterMark in negative area. Wait two minutes. Apply chalk with cosmetic sponge.
4. Lay the negative area of the mask over patterned paper; cut out background, trim to fit ATC.
5. Apply glue to the back surface of the paper; align with image. Burnish in position with bone folder.
6. Use PITT pen to clean up and darken outlines. Round corners; accent edges with colored pencil.

Honeysuckle and Fleur Fly

Janet Klein

MATERIALS

Rubber Stamps: Fleur Fly Butterflies, Flower Background and Flower Words Block by Stampotique Originals

Dye Inkpads: Ancient Page Black

Papers: Cardstock; Patterned Papers

Paints: Watercolors; Green Acrylic Paint

Markers/Pens: PITT Artist Pen

Other: Craft Wire; Foam Tape

Tools: Small Tip Water Brush by Ninji; Post-it Note

INSTRUCTIONS

1. Stamp Fleur Fly stamp, paint with watercolor and cut out. Bend wire for antenna.
2. Mask part of ATC, stamp flower background on top portion. Mask again and stamp flower type on other half of ATC. Cover one-half of ATC with Post-it Note, paint with watercolors.
3. Adhere strips of paper on bottom half allowing flower type to peek through as shown.
4. Adhere butterfly with foam tape and sandwich in wire antennae. Edge with acrylic paint.

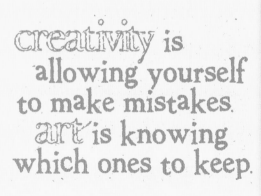

creativity is allowing yourself to make mistakes. art is knowing which ones to keep.

Arty
Janet Klein

MATERIALS
Rubber Stamps: Arty by Stampotique Originals

Dye Inkpads: Ancient Page Black

Papers: Cardstock

Paints: Watercolors; Twinkling H20's

Colored Pencils: Prismacolor

Pens: PITT Artist Pen

Other: Rhinestones

Tools: Hole Punch; Water Brush

INSTRUCTIONS
1. Stamp image, paint with watercolors and Twinkling H20's; go over lines with PITT pen.
2. Paint swatches of Twinkling H20's on scrap paper.
3. Punch scrap paper, glue punched pieces to ATC; add rhinestones over some of the dots.

A Bird in the Grass
Janet Klein

MATERIALS
Rubber Stamps: Bird and Heart Border by Stampotique Originals

Dye Inkpads: Archival Jet Black

Papers: Cardstock; Magazine

Paints: Gouache

Colored Pencils: Prismacolor

Markers/Pens: PITT Artist Pens

Tools: Small Tip Water Brush by Ninji

INSTRUCTIONS
1. Stamp heart border, leaving area for bird image. Stamp bird. Paint images with fine tip Ninji water brush and gouache.
2. Layer and accent additional colors with colored pencils. Scribble in the background.
3. Glue two small strips of type onto borders. Complete the border with alternating blocks of colors and PITT pen. Accent black line work with fine-tipped PITT pen.
4. Snip small strips of paper to create faux clippings, adhere to card.

Sun Outside My Window
Janet Klein

MATERIALS
Rubber Stamps: Flower Background, Text and Type and Sun by Stampotique Originals

Dye Inkpads: Ancient Page Sage and Plum Wine

Papers: Watercolor Paper

Paints: Watercolors; Twinkling H20's

Markers/Pens: PITT Artist Pen

Other: Craft Wire; Eyelet; Charm

Tools: Xacto Knife; Eyelet Setter; 1/16" Hole Punch; Sewing Machine; Water Brush by Ninji

INSTRUCTIONS
1. Stamp sun image on ATC. Mask part of ATC, stamp flower block, stamp text/type block on the remaining bottom space.
2. Use watercolors accented with Twinkling H20's to paint background. Paint sun with Twinkling H20's.
3. Cut out a circular center in ATC. Paint a deeper shade of green in a border around opening.
4. Use fine PITT pen to outline circular opening and create a checked pattern alternating with the green. Center sun behind opening, adhere.
5. Sew edges on sewing machine. Leave strings hanging.
6. Paint variegated colors to create a border.
7. Set eyelet, twist wire, add charm and hang from eyelet.

Giggle and Calla

Janet Klein

MATERIALS

Rubber Stamps: Giggle and Calla by Stampotique Originals

Dye Inkpads: Archival Jet Black

Papers: Cardstock; Patterned Paper; Newsprint

Paints: Watercolors; Twinkling H20's

Colored Pencils: Prismacolor

Markers/Pens: PITT Artist Pen; Soufflé Pens by Sakura

Tools: Heat Tool; Xacto Knife; Corner Rounder; Water Brush by Ninji

INSTRUCTIONS

1. Stamp ribbon border stamp twice vertically and horizontally to create a window in the center, cut out window with Xacto knife.
2. Stamp word "giggle", color with Twinkling H2Os. Stamp fleur fly image, color with pencils.
3. Hand paint stripes in two of the corner spaces as shown.
4. Trace the remaining spaces, cut out shapes and use as patterns to cut out scraps of paper and book text to glue in spaces as shown, color.
5. Color ribbon borders with pencils and Soufflé pens. Glue fleur fly image in window. Use PITT pen to freshen the ink on all edges.
6. Round corners, edge with pencil.

Bowed Belle(s)

Janet Klein

MATERIALS

Rubber Stamps: Fleur Bell by Stampotique Originals

Dye Inkpads: Ancient Page Black and Palm Leaf

Papers: Cardstock

Paints: Watercolors; Twinkling H2O's

Markers/Pens: PITT Artist Pen

Pencils: Prismacolor

Other: Ribbon; Foam Tape

Tools: Water Brush by Ninji; Corner Punch; Xacto

INSTRUCTIONS (for card below)

1. Stamp Fleur Bell, stamp again to make a mask, cut out and cover image.
2. Paint with watercolors and Twinkling H2O's. Scribble pencil on card, using a darker color around the edge.
3. Cut horizontal slits along the right side of ATC. Feed ribbon in and out of openings, glue ends of ribbon behind card.

INSTRUCTIONS

1. Stamp image, stamp again on book text.
2. Spray type with eucalyptus spray ink, wipe with sponge to create a stain. Cut out stamped image from stained paper. Save the remaining negative space.
3. Stamp bottom of image on scrap paper. Trim out positive area and set aside negative shape for bottom of ATC card.
4. Color image with watercolors and twinkling H2Os.
5. Apply glue to the back surface of the negative space text and scrap papers, align around the image, burnish in place.
6. Paint stripes with watercolor on open portion of the card.
7. Apply acrylic paints in an alternating pattern.
8. Use PITT pen to clean up all edges. Round edges; add a loose accent of colored pencil line to the edges of the type to blend in with the colors of the card.

Hiya Cinth and Fleur Girl

Janet Klein

MATERIALS

Rubber Stamps: Hiya and Fluer Girl by Stampotique Originals
Dye Inkpads: Archival Jet Black
Papers: Cardstock; Book Text
Colored Pencils: Prismacolor

Paints: Acrylics; Watercolors; Twinkling H2O's
Other: Eucalyptus Ink; Antiquing Solution
Tools: Cosmetic Sponge; Corner Rounder; Water Brush by Ninji

Brown-Eyed Susan

Janet Klein

MATERIALS

Rubber Stamps: Stampotique Originals
Dye Inkpads: Archival Black
Paper: Cardstock; Scrap of Astrobright
Paints: Watercolors; Gouache
Colored Pencils: Prismacolor
Markers/Pens: PITT Artist Pen
Other: Embroidery Floss,
Tools: 1/16" Hole Punch; Corner Rounder; Water Brush by Ninji

INSTRUCTIONS

1. Stamp image, mask all but a small section for gatepost. Stamp side pillar portion of gate stamp.
2. Stamp gate on scrap watercolor paper, paint and cut out.
3. Stamp mid-section of stamp on pink paper, cut out dress.
4. Paint arms, face, sky, and ground with watercolors. Shadow gate sections.
5. Use thinned gouache for hair. Glue the dress piece in place.
6. Align gate, make a crease on left portion of gate so that it will open, adhere.
7. Trim corners. Punch holes; sew embroidery floss through holes. Use PITT pen to clean up edges.

Gone Preppy

Janet Klein

MATERIALS:

Rubber Stamps: Carol's Flower; Flowers Background and Text Block by Stampotique Originals

Papers: Cardstock; Watercolor Paper

Dye Inkpads: Ancient Page Sage and Plum Wine

Paints: Watercolors; Twinkling H2O's

Colored Pencils: Prismacolor

Other: Ribbon

Tools: Foam Tape; Water Brush by Ninji

INSTRUCTIONS

1. Stamp Carol's Flower on watercolor paper, cut out.
2. Mask half of ATC, stamp small flowers background. Mask and stamp flower text on bottom.
3. Use watercolors accented with Twinkling H2Os to paint as shown.
4. Adhere flower to cardstock, cut out leaving border around flower. Attach with foam tape.
5. Tie ribbons and attach, accent edges with pencils.

China Belle

Janet Klein

MATERIALS

Rubber Stamps: China Belle by Stampotique Originals

Pigment Inkpads: VersaMark WaterMark

Dye Inkpads: Archival Black

Papers: Cardstock; Patterned Paper; Joss Paper

Paints: Watercolors; Gouache; Twinkling H2O's

Pastels/Chalks: Various Chalks

Colored Pencils: Prismacolor

Markers/Pens: PITT Artist Pen

Other: Embroidery Floss; Craft Wire

Tools: Cosmetic Sponge; Heat Tool; Corner Rounder; 1/8" Hole Punch; Water Brush by Ninji

INSTRUCTIONS

1. Stamp China Belle image on ATC, stamp again on scrap paper, cut out, keep positive image for mask. Stamp top of image on patterned paper, cut out.
2. Apply watercolor wash to face, neck, and hands. Paint kimono with Twinkling H2O's. Paint hair petals with gouache. Paint robe stripe with watercolor.
3. Mask image; press background with VersaMark pad in negative area. Wait two minutes. Apply chalks with sponge. Add scraps of joss paper.
4. Apply glue to the back surface of the patterned paper, align image, burnish.
5. Punch hole and add hand made tassel as shown
6. Use PITT pen to clean up and darken edges. Round corners, accent edges with pencil.

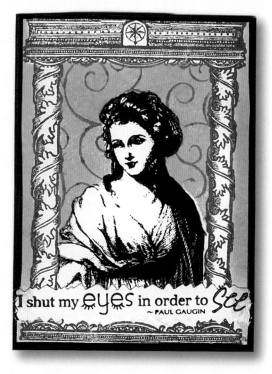

Birds of a Feather

Sue Roddis

MATERIALS

Rubber Stamps: Tags, Birds Nest and Blackbird by Invoke Art; Trailing Vine by Hero Arts; ATC Circle by Catslife Press

Dye Inkpads: Memories Black; Adirondack Oregano

Papers: Cardstock

Other: Water Soluble Crayons by Lyra; Metal Letters by Making Memories; Feathers; Ribbon; Safety Pins; Eyelet; Judkins Diamond Glaze; Tags

Tools: Heat Tool

INSTRUCTIONS

1. Color cardstock with crayons; blend with water.
2. Stamp nest and blackbird images, color with watercolor crayons. Stamp trailing vine.
3. Stamp tags, color, cut out and attach to ATCs with safety pins, add feathers.
4. Add ribbons and letters, mount on cardstock.

ATC Shrine

Dawn Binyon

MATERIALS

Rubber Stamps: Maiden #1 by Paper Inspirations; ATC Shrine by Lost Coast Designs; Swirls and Curls by Stampabilities; Pixie Expressions by PSX

Dye Inkpads: Marvy Matchable Pale Violet, Violet and Orchid; StazOn Jet Black

Papers: Glossy Cardstock

INSTRUCTIONS

1. Mask outer edges of ATC, stamp woman image. Stamp again, cut out to make a mask.
2. Cover image, stipple over top, stamp swirl image.
3. Stamp shrine, then mask outer edges and stipple. Adhere quote.

Time To Go
Judith Godwin

MATERIALS

Rubber Stamps: Pocket Watch by PSX; Watch Parts by Postmodern Design; Three Piece Pocket Watch by Inkadinkado; X-V-I by Art Impressions

Dye Inkpads: Archival Jet Black and Sepia; Distress Ink

Papers: Cardstock

Markers/Pens: Gold Paint Pen by Krylon

Other: Office RUSH Stamp; Watch Face; Watch Glass; Mosaic Stickers; Key; Button; Ticket; Judikins Diamond Glaze

INSTRUCTIONS:

1. Crumple ATC, rub distress ink over creases. Iron paper flat Randomly stamp watch images.
2. Stamp pocket watch, distress and cut out. Edge with paint pen, adhere watch glass over watch face.
3. Cut tag, punch hole; string and knot. Stamp RUSH on tag.
4. Adhere key and button.

Is Anybody There?
Judith Godwin

MATERIALS

Rubber Stamps: Telephone and Hello by Rubbermoon

Pigment Inkpads: Brilliance Graphic Black

Dye Inkpads: Archival Sepia

Papers: Cardstock; Mulberry Paper; Catalog Page

Other: Craft Wire; Hole Punch; Clear Embossing Powder; Conversation Bubble

Tools: Peircing tool

INSTRUCTIONS

1. Stamp and emboss phone, cut out. Adhere to mulberry paper.
2. Curl wire for phone, poke holes and attach.
3. Stamp word "hello" twice on conversation bubble, distress edges.

In The Family Room
Judith Godwin

MATERIALS

Rubber Stamps: Woman by B Line Designs; Spindle and Passion Definition by Postmodern Design

Dye Inkpads: Archival Jet Black; Archival Sepia

Papers: Cardstock; Doll House

Markers/Pens: Tombow

Other: Ribbon; Vintage Photos; Frames; Transparency

INSTRUCTIONS

1. Adhere floor and wallpaper to ATC. Stamp woman image, color, cut out.
2. Stamp passion definition, tear out, distress.
3. Adhere woman and definition to ATC.
4. Trim vintage photos to fit frames. Cut transparency to fit frames, tie ribbons to frames.

Face in the Window
Judy Godwin

MATERIALS

Rubber Stamps: Ink Bottle by A Stamp in the Hand; Frame by Northwoods; Collaged Woman by Acey Duecy; Art Label by Catslife Press; Crackle by Renaissance Art Stamps; Word Collage by PSX; Date Stamp (generic)

Pigment Inkpads: Brilliance Graphite Black; VersaMagic Malted Mauve; ColorBox Red Pepper

Dye Inkpads: Archival Sepia; Mustard Distress Ink

Markers/Pens: Marvy Markers

Other: Post-it Note

Tools: Stipple Brush; Xacto Knife; Corner Rounder; Puzzle Piece Punch by The Punch Bunch

INSTRUCTIONS

1. Stamp collaged figure on cardstock in black ink. Color mouth with red marker.
2. Stamp figure again on Post-it and cut out for mask. Mask image, softly stipple Malted Mauve ink around figure. Remove mask.
3. Stamp oval ink image and the date in red.
4. Stipple a scrap of text with Mustard ink and punch out puzzle piece. Glue puzzle over focus image.
5. Stamp "ART" on tag and adhere.
6. Stamp and trim square frame on one side of cardstock and crackle on the reverse side as shown, slit center. Fold out and adhere face behind frame.

Black Family Album
Judith Godwin

MATERIALS

Rubber Stamps: Original Definitions Family by Hero Arts

Dye Inkpads: Archival Jet Black, Mustard and Sepia

Papers: Adhesive-Backed Glossy Paper; Bond Paper; Black Cardstock

Pens/Markers: Krylon Silver Paint Pen

Other: Vintage Photos; Flower Charm

Tools: Deckle Edge Scissors; Sponge

INSTRUCTIONS

1. Trim photos and adhere to black cardstock cut to ATC size, add corners.
2. Sponge and age adhesive glossy paper with Mustard ink; allow to dry. Stamp Definitions in sepia. Cut out words and glue to ATC.
3. Write date with paint pen and add flower charm.

Beauty
Roben-Marie Smith

MATERIALS

Rubber Stamps: Beauty by Paperbag Studios

Pigment Inkpads: VersaFine Onyx Black

Papers: Li'l Davis Designs

Other: Ribbon; Brad; Silk Flower; Bubble Letter and Circle Clip by Li'l Davis Designs

Tools: 1/16" Hole Punch

INSTRUCTIONS

1. Stamp image, add flower with brad.
2. Place bubble letter "B" into circle clip. Tie ribbons to end and slide onto card.

Joy

Roben-Marie Smith

MATERIALS

Rubber Stamps: The Chair by Paperbag Studios

Pigment Inkpads: VersaFine Onyx Black

Papers: K&Company; NRN Designs

Other: Word "joy" by K&Company; Button; Ribbon

INSTRUCTIONS

1. Stamp chair image on patterned paper, adhere word "joy".
2. Add ribbon and button.

Just a Note
Roben-Marie Smith

MATERIALS

Rubber Stamps: Buttons by Paperbag Studios

Dye Inkpads: Adirondack Eggplant

Papers: Book Text; Paper Loft

Paints: Yellow Acrylic

Other: Word by Li'l Davis Designs; Ribbon; Button

INSTRUCTIONS

1. Stamp button image.
2. Tear scrap of text paper, adhere embellishment as shown.

Sweet Pea
Roben-Marie Smith

MATERIALS

Rubber Stamps: Sweet Pea by Paperbag Studios

Pigment Inkpads: VersaFine Onyx Black

Papers: BasicGrey; Reminisce

Other: Ribbon; Ribbon Charm by 7gypsies

INSTRUCTIONS

1. Stamp sweet pea image, cut out and adhere.
2. Cut ribbon, thread with ribbon charm; adhere.

Enjoy Pears
Roben-Marie Smith

MATERIALS
Rubber Stamps: Script Pear by Paperbag Studios
Pigment Inkpads: VersaFine Onyx Black
Papers: The Paper Loft
Markers/Pens: PITT Artist Pen
Other: Rub-Ons by Making Memories; Eyelets; Crayon; Ribbons; Waxed Thread
Tools: 1/8" Hole Punch; Eyelet Setter

INSTRUCTIONS
1. Adhere patterned paper to ATC.
2. Stamp pear image, outline with crayon.
3. Set eyelets, run thread through eyelets, tie.
4. Draw lines around outside of ATC with PITT Pen, rub on word "enjoy".

Every Step
Roben-Marie Smith

MATERIALS
Rubber Stamps: Every Step by Paperbag Studios; Corner Stamps by Making Memories
Pigment Inkpads: VersaFine Onyx Black
Dye Inkpads: Adirondack Mushroom
Papers: BasicGrey
Other: Elastic by 7gypsies; Ribbons; Eyelets
Tools: 1/8" Hole Punch; Eyelet Setter

INSTRUCTIONS
1. Randomly stamp corners on background to distress. Stamp image over background.
2. Punch holes, set eyelets.
3. Attach elastic to card through holes. Tie ribbons and thread to elastic.

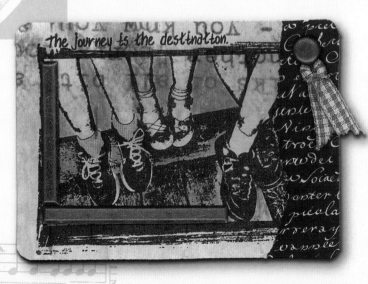

The Journey
Roben-Marie Smith

MATERIALS
Rubber Stamps: The Journey by Paperbag Studios
Dye Inkpads: StazOn Jet Black
Papers: Autumn Leaves; 7gypsies
Colored Pencils: Watercolor Pencils
Other: Brad Bar by Karen Foster Designs; Blender Pen; Ribbon
Tools: 1/8" Hole Punch

INSTRUCTIONS
1. Stamp image on patterned paper, color as shown; blend with pen.
2. Tear small piece of coordinating paper and adhere.
3. Write title with PITT pen.
4. Punch hole and add ribbon tied to brad.
5. Add brad bars.

One Fish Two Fish

Janet Klein

MATERIALS

Rubber Stamps: Fish Images by Stampotique Originals

Dye Inkpads: Archival Jet Black

Papers: Patterned Paper; Book Text

Paints: Watercolors

Colored Pencils: Prismacolor

Markers/Pens: PITT Artist Pen

Other: Ribbon; Beads

Tools: Xacto Knife; Cutting Mat; Hole Punch; Water Brush by Ninji

INSTRUCTIONS

1. Copy, reduce and cut out text from book, color as shown.
2. Stamp fish images; stamp additional on patterned paper as shown. Cut out image to use negative space as background.
3. Color fish in hues of green. Go over black lines with PITT pen where needed.
4. Center fish opening in paper over corresponding fish, glue and burnish.
5. Cut pieces of colored text and glue randomly to frame the card.
6. String beads on short length of ribbon. Punch holes and slip ribbon through holes, secure to back. Adhere cardstock over ribbon backs to hide.
7. Touch edges with a few strokes of white pencil.

Under the Sea

Janet Klein

MATERIALS

Rubber Stamps: Fish Images by Stampotique Originals

Dye Inkpads: Archival Black

Papers: 140 lb. Watercolor Paper

Paints: Watercolors

Colored Pencils: Prismacolor

Markers/Pens: PITT Artist Pen

Other: Glitter Glue Pens; Fibers; Salt

Tools: Water Brush by Ninji

INSTRUCTIONS

1. Stamp fish images; dampen the negative space around fish. Fill in background with watercolors as shown.
2. Sprinkle wet wash with table salt, remove salt when dry.
3. Paint fish images. Add swirls and loose lines of glitter glue to the background.
4. Cut fibers to fit the edges of the ATC, adhere.
5. Highlight fish with colored pencils.

Seaside Beauties

Jane Maley

MATERIALS

Rubber Stamps: Bathing Beauties by The Queen's Dresser Drawers

Dye Inkpads: StazOn Timber Brown and Saddle Brown

Paper: Glossy Cardstock

Other: Alphabet Stickers by Making Memories; JudiKins Diamond Glaze by; Starfish; Alcohol Inks

INSTRUCTIONS

1. Drop alcohol inks onto a small area of cardstock; place ATC face down in inks, swirl to coat. Allow to dry.
2. Stamp Bathing Beauties in brown inks, distress edges of card.
3. Adhere starfish and alphabet letters.

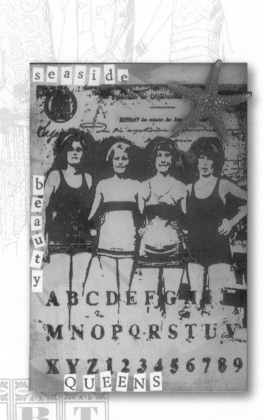

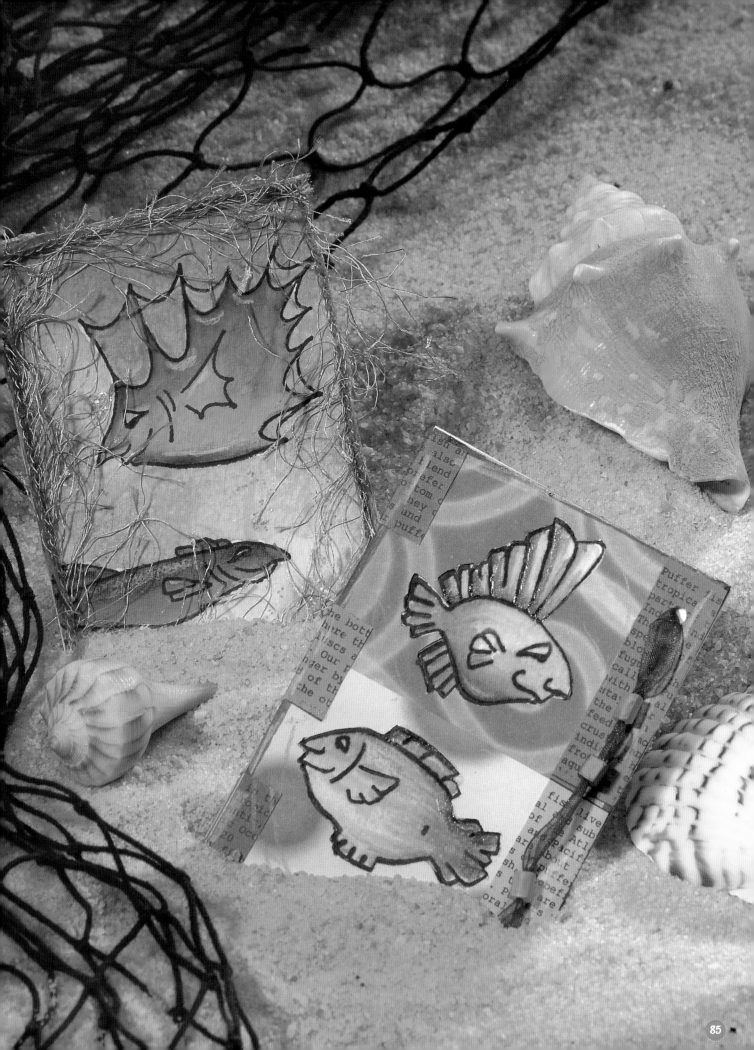

Exotic

Amy Wellenstein

MATERIALS

Rubber Stamps: Graffiti Alphabet by Stampotique Originals; Text by Acey Deucy; Dots by Hot Potatoes; Floral Background by JudiKins; Face by The Moon Rose

Pigment Inkpads: VersaMark WaterMark; VersaFine Onyx Black

Dye Inkpads: Archival Carnation

Papers: Cardstock

Pastels/Chalks: Various Chalks

INSTRUCTIONS

1. Stamp face image, stamp again on scratch paper. Cut out to make a mask.
2. Mask over the image, overstamp floral background with VersaMark WaterMark. Wait two minutes.
3. With mask still in place, color background with chalks.
4. Remove mask, color focal image.
5. Stamp word "exotic" and dots as shown.

Beauty

Amy Wellenstein

MATERIALS

Rubber Stamps: Phone Booth Beauty, Antique Border and "beauty" by Stampotique Originals; Large Cancellation and Christmas Cube by Stampington & Company

Pigment Inkpads: VersaMark WaterMark; VersaFine Onyx Black

Paper: Cardstock

Pastels/Chalks: Various Chalks

INSTRUCTIONS

1. Stamp woman image on ATC, stamp three more times to create masks.
2. Cut one mask of the entire image with a square border, cut one mask for the negative, and the last mask of just the woman.
3. Apply the negative and woman masks, overstamp with Christmas text in black ink.
4. Remove masks and color the woman's face with chalks.
5. Apply whole image mask, overstamp with cancellation using VersaMark WaterMark. Wait two minutes
6. With the mask still in place, color background with chalks as shown.
7. Remove the mask and color background.

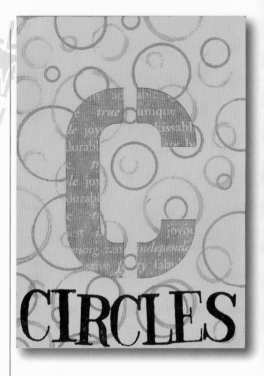

Stencil Circles

Amy Wellenstein

MATERIALS

Rubber Stamps: Circles by Stampotique Originals; Alphabet Stamps by Ephemera Design Studio

Dye Inkpads: Adirondack Ginger; India Ink Black by Stewart Superior

Papers: Creative Imaginations

Paints: Yellow and Pink Acrylic

Other: Stencil

INSTRUCTIONS

1. Paint "C" stencil in yellow.
2. Stamp Circles in Ginger ink. Overstamp circles with pink acrylic paint.
3. Stamp word "circles" in black.
4. Layer pink script paper so it can be seen on the face of the stencil.

Otto ATC

Amy Wellenstein

MATERIALS

Rubber Stamps: Otto, Fax to Wolfgang and Antique Border by Stampotique Originals; Dots in Circles by Hot Potatoes; Deux, Trois and Quatre (source unknown)

Pigment Inkpads: VersaMark WaterMark; VersaFine Onyx Black

Dye Inkpads: Adirondack Butterscotch

Paper: Cardstock

Pastels/Chalks: Various Chalks

INSTRUCTIONS

1. Stamp Otto on ATC, stamp again to create a mask.
2. Mask the image and overstamp with dots using VersaMark WaterMark. Wait two minutes.
3. With the mask still in place, color the background, then overstamp with text.
4. Remove the mask and color the focal image.
5. Stamp border on sides and words in circles.

Stencil Stripes

Amy Wellenstein

MATERIALS

Rubber Stamps: Thin Stripes by The Cat's Pajamas; Alphabetic Border by Limited Edition; Alphabet Stamps by Ephemera Design Studio

Dye Inkpads: Archival Aqua; India Ink Black by Stewart Superior

Papers: Creative Imaginations

Paints: Aquamarine and Orange Acrylic

Other: Stencil

INSTRUCTIONS:

1. Paint "S" stencil, stamp with stripe image.
2. Stamp alphabetic border as shown, stamp word "stripes",
3. Layer teal paper so it can be seen on the face of the stencil.

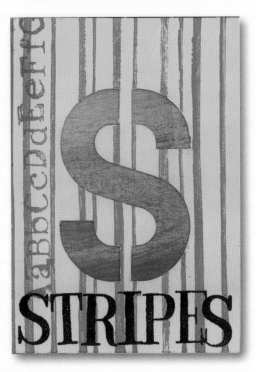

Stencil Dots

Amy Wellenstein

MATERIALS

Rubber Stamps: Antique Description and Dots by Stampotique Originals; Alphabet Stamps by Ephemera Design Studio

Dye Inkpads: Archival Aqua; India Ink Black by Stewart Superior

Papers: Creative Imaginations

Paint: Making Memories Aquamarine and Honeydew

Other: Stencil

INSTRUCTIONS

1. Paint "D" stencil, stamp dots.
2. Stamp description over the stencil. Stamp word "dots".
3. Layer patterned paper behind stencil.

friends are like flowers

Ti Amo

Dawn Binyon

MATERIALS

Rubber Stamps: Postoid by Stampabilities; Pisa by A Country Welcome; Passport by Limited Edition; Ti Amo by Josie Cirincione for Stampotique Originals

Dye Inkpads: Marvy Matchables Light Brown, Dark Brown, Ochre and Burnt Umber

Papers: Cardstock; Mulberry Papers; Manila File Folder

Tools: Notched Corner Punch

INSTRUCTIONS

1. For wood grain effect, hold stamp pad at 45-degree angle and gently glide across glossy paper, repeat with several shades of brown.
2. Stamp images on ATC, stamp postoid image on file folder, punch out.
3. Layer manila image with brown background scrap and mulberry paper.
4. Notch corners, stamp words "Ti Amo".

I Shut My eyes

Dawn Binyon

MATERIALS

Rubber Stamps: Dream by Stampers Anonymous; Small Postcard and Envelope by A Country Welcome; Pixie Expressions by PSX; Eye Stamp (hand-carved with Staedtler Mastercarve Block designed by Dawn Binyon)

Dye Inkpads: StazOn Jet Black and Cotton White

Papers: Cardstock; Pink Tissue Paper

Paints: Watercolors

Other: Silver Aluminum Tape; Tracing Wheel; Collage Unleashed by Traci Bautista

INSTRUCTIONS

1. Paint tissue with watercolors. Dry. Adhere papers together, dry again.
2. Stamp images directly to layered papers.
3. Finish edges with metal tape. Run tracing wheel over tape.

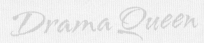

Last Kiss

Dawn Binyon

MATERIALS

Rubber Stamps: Last Kiss by Eclectic Omnibus; Priceless by River City Rubberworks; Swirls and Curls by Stampabilities; Posy Queen by Stampers Anonymous

Pigment Inkpads: ColorBox Warm Violet, Wisteria and Dark Peony

Dye Inkpads: StazOn Jet Black

Papers: Glossy Cardstock

Tools: Heat Tool

INSTRUCTIONS

1. Stamp swirl background image, heat set.
2. Run stamp pads randomly over ATC.
3. Stamp Last Kiss and Priceless; cut out and adhere to ATC.

Sea
Andrea Robert

MATERIALS

Rubber Stamps: Sea Waves by The Stampsmith; Background Shells by PSX; Shrink-It Shell (source unknown)

Pigment Inkpads: Encore Ultimate Metallic Teal

Dye Inkpads: Adirondack Stream and Caramel

Papers: White Tissue Paper; Blue Mulberry Paper; White Cardstock

Markers/Pens: Marvy Metallic Blue Marker; Blue Glitter Gel Pen

Other: Blue Embossing Powder; Aleene's Shrink-It-Sheet by Duncan; Book Page

Tools: Heat Tool; Toaster Oven

INSTRUCTIONS

1. Cut out or stamp quote. Lightly stamp shells image on quote. Heat set and trim.
2. Stamp, emboss and trim waves image. Add to bottom of quote. Layer onto cardstock.
3. Add sand dollar embellishment made from Shrink-It Sheet.

Frida Kahlo
Dawn Binyon

MATERIALS

Rubber Stamps: Frida Postage Stamp by A Stamp in the Hand; Famous Artist Signatures by JudiKins; Pixie Expressions by PSX

Dye Inkpads: VersaFine Onyx Black

Markers/Pens: Marvy Manganese Blue, Caribbean Blue, Blue, Black Red and Pale Orange Markers

Papers: Cardstock; Mulberry Paper

Tools: Decorative Edge Scissors

INSTRUCTIONS

1. Ink Frida directly on the stamp using markers.
2. Stamp Famous Signatures on blue background and cut with decorative scissors.
3. Mount on white background, layer Frida on top.
4. Stamp saying in black ink on mulberry paper and attach.

Walk in the Park
Dawn Binyon

MATERIALS

Rubber Stamps: Ladies by A Country Welcome; Manuscript XV by Cherry Pie; Feather by Eclectic Omnibus; Art Stamp by Catslife Press; Background Music by Penny Black; Text by A Stamp in the Hand

Pigment Inkpads: ColorBox Bisque, Burnt Sienna, Creamy Brown, Chestnut Roan and Dark Brown

Dye Inkpads: StazOn Jet Black and Timber Brown

Papers: Cardstock

Tools: Heat Tool

Other: Tile by EK Success; Shipping Tag; Fibers

INSTRUCTIONS

1. Stamp first background image, heat set.
2. Run ATC randomly over inkpads.
3. Stamp manila tag, add fibers, attach. Stamp word "art", attach.

Psyche
Carlene Federer

MATERIALS

Rubber Stamps: Face by Inkadinkado

Pigment Inkpads: StazOn Jet Black; ColorBox Paint Box

Other: Vintage Dictionary Paper; Embossing Powder; Rhinestone; Glitter

Tools: Heat Tool

INSTRUCTIONS

1. Rub ATC over several colors of ink for background.
2. Stamp woman and wings images; add glitter, heat set.
3. Add dictionary definition and black rhinestone to finish.

Barbie
Jill Haglund

MATERIALS

Rubber Stamps: Vogue by Tim Holtz for Stampers Anonymous

Dye Inkpads: Black India Ink by Stewart Superior

Papers: Cardstock

Paints: Twinkling H2O's

Pastels/Chalks: Neoart Wax Pastels by Caran d'Ache

Other: Pink Flowers Brad; Ribbon; Staples

Tools: Small Watercolor Brush

INSTRUCTIONS

1. Stamp image and cut out.
2. Paint ATC with Twinkling H2O's, then add touches of pastels.
3. Attach brads, adhere stamped image and staple ribbon to finish.

Butterfly Queen
Jill Haglund

MATERIALS

Rubber Stamps: Heart Song by Tim Holtz for Stampers Anonymous

Dye Inkpads: Black India Ink by Stewart Superior

Papers: Yellow Text-Weight Paper; Newsprint

Paints: Titan Buff by Golden; Twinkling H2O's

Pastels/Chalks: Neoart Wax Pastels by Caran d'Ache

Colored Pencils: Watercolor Pencils

Other: Glitter Glue; Playing Card

Tools: Small Watercolor Brush

INSTRUCTIONS

1. Adhere text paper to card. Add newsprint, then apply diluted paint.
2. Stamp image and cut out; paint with colored pencils and Twinkling H2O's.
3. Create border with pastels, then add randomly smudges and scribble as shown.
4. Add glitter glue to tip of crown to finish.

You're Invited
Jill Haglund

MATERIALS

Rubber Stamps: Peddler's Pack Stampworks

Pigment Inkpads: ColorBox Orchid and Blue

Dye Inkpads: VersaFine Onyx Black

Colored Pencils: Prismacolor Blue, Yellow and Pink

Other: Word Stickers by Making Memories; Glitter

Tools: Paper Cutter

INSTRUCTIONS

1. Apply pigment ink to blank ATC.
2. Stamp image, color with pencils. Add glitter to crowns to finish.

We Are Not Amused
Carlene Federer

MATERIALS

Rubber Stamps: Swirl by Heidi Swapp; We Are Not Amused by River City Rubberworks

Dye Inkpads: Archival PLum

Papers: Cardstock

Other: Image and Crown by ARTchix Studio; Rhinestone

INSTRUCTIONS

1. Stamp swirl on back of ATC, add image.
2. Glue crown onto image, add rhinestone.
3. Stamp "We are not amused" to finish.

Heart
Roben-Marie Smith

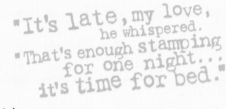

MATERIALS
Rubber Stamps: Ruled Alphabet by Paperbag Studios
Dye Inkpads: Adirondack Oregano
Papers: Chalk Motif and Strawberry Cream by BasicGrey
Other: Ribbon; Metal Alphabets by Making Memories; Steel End by 7gypsies; Thumbtack Brad by Karen Foster Designs; Distressed Metal Heart
Tools: Hole Punch

INSTRUCTIONS
1. Adhere papers to card, stamp image.
2. Adhere heart to steel end with ribbon. Attach steel end to ATC with brad.
3. Spell word "Love" with metal alphabet.

Thrive
Roben-Marie Smith

MATERIALS
Rubber Stamps: Addison by Paperbag Studios
Dye Inkpads: VersaFine Onyx Black; Distress Ink
Papers: BasicGrey
Other: Metal Alphabet Letters by Making Memories; Brad Bar by Karen Foster Designs; Book Paper
Tools: Sponge; 1/16" Hole Punch

INSTRUCTIONS
1. Glue paper to card, stamp image.
2. Distress edges of book paper with ink and adhere as shown.
3. Punch holes and add brad bar, add cut out metal letters.

"It's late, my love, he whispered. "That's enough stamping for one night... it's time for bed."

Smile
Roben-Marie Smith

MATERIALS
Rubber Stamps: Smile by Paperbag Studios; Definition by Stampotique Originals
Dye Inkpads: VersaFine Onyx Black
Papers: Cherry Pie by BasicGrey
Other: Printed Twill by 7gypsies; Ribbon; Buttons by Making Memories; Playing Card; Foam Tape

INSTRUCTIONS
1. Stamp definition image along edges of card; stamp part of smile image.
2. Glue trim to card; add cut out smile image and buttons.

Friends
Roben-Marie Smith

MATERIALS
Rubber Stamps: Miss by Paperbag Studios
Dye Inkpads: VersaFine Onyx Black
Papers: BasicGrey
Other: Ribbon by K&Company; Tags by BasicGrey; Eyelets; "Friends" Adhesive Word; Playing Card
Tools: Dymo Label Maker; Eyelet Setter; 1/8" Hole Punch

INSTRUCTIONS
1. Stamp image on tag and attach to card.
2. Punch holes and set eyelets; tie ribbons through eyelets.
3. Adhere "friends" adhesive word to card to finish.

Bliss
Roben-Marie Smith

MATERIALS
Rubber Stamps: Daisy Trio by Paperbag Studios
Dye Inkpads: Adirondack Raisin
Papers: Red Corrugated Cardstock; Smooth Red Cardstock; Light Pink Cardstock
Paints: White Acrylic
Other: Rub-On Words by Making Memories; Metal Frame by K&Company
Tools: Paintbrush; Heat Tool

INSTRUCTIONS
1. Dry brush corrugated cardstock with acrylic paint.
2. Apply paint to image and stamp on cardstock.
3. Rub on word "bliss", adhere under frame as shown, attach to ATC.

abcdefgh

abcdefgh

klmnopq

stuvwxy

LOVE

connection! But, yes, it is the dream of self.

t H R i v e

Adore, worship, idolize:
appreciate.

joy \ jôi \ n.   of happiness an

smile

attachment,

bliss

FRIENDS

Patterns

(Instructions for all Patterns ATCs)

Judith Godwin

MATERIALS

Rubber Stamps: Pattern and Stickpins by B Line Designs; Details by Postscript Studios

Dye Inkpads: Archival Jet Black

Papers: Cardstock in Desired Colors; Pattern Tissue

Other: Eyelets; Charms; Sequin Pins; Fabric; Floss; Buttons; Package of Snaps; Pattern

Tools: 1/16" Hole Punch

INSTRUCTIONS

1. Stamp pattern on tissue for each ATC, cut out, then cut in half.
2. Apply fabric to ATCs using double-sided tape. Fold corners and sides of fabric in toward center; tape to secure.
3. Pin pattern with sequin pins through fabric only, about 8-9 pins per pattern half; add eyelets.
4. Shrink pattern, cut out mini pattern envelopes; glue edges together, add eyelets. Tie pattern envelopes to fabric and through eyelets with floss.
5. Cut out small tags and add silver eyelets and buttons.
6. Write "5¢ Buttons" on tag. Add charms, buttons and snaps.
7. Make embroidery floss skeins and cover with gold cardstock, adhere elements as shown.

Row Houses

Janet Klein

MATERIALS

Rubber Stamps: Row Houses by Stampotique Originals

Dye Inkpads: Archival Jet Black

Papers: White Cardstock; Paper Scraps

Colored Pencils: Prismacolor

Paints: Watercolors

Markers/Pens: PITT Artist Pen

Tools: Corner Rounder; Small Tip Ninji Water Brush

INSTRUCTIONS

1. Stamp Row Houses image on cardstock. Stamp image again on a variety of about four different papers. Stamp image again, cut out to make a mask.
2. Cut out roofs and doors from assorted papers.
3. Paint desired areas in watercolors with Ninji water brush. Apply another layer of watercolor to create patterns in the sky and grasses.
4. Add doors and roofs as shown. Round corners of ATC, color edges with pencils.
5. Randomly scribble to the edges of the type; use PITT pen to create accents.

Refuge

Christy Hawkins

MATERIALS

Rubber Stamps: Cat stamp from Magenta, Music stamp from Great Impressions Rubber Stamps

Dye Inkpads: Memories Black by Stewart Superior

Papers: Cardstock and Vellum

Colored Pencils: Prismacolor Pencils

Other: Post-It-Note; Computer font: CK Journaling from Creating Keepsakes; Xyron Adhesive (for the vellum)

Tools: Xyron machine

INSTRUCTIONS

1. Cut and layer black and gold cardstock as shown.
2. Tear post-It and mask left side of the card. Stamp cat image in black on right half of ATC. Color wth Prismacolor pencils.
3. Print the quote "There are two means of refuge from the miseries of life: music and cats." by Albert Schweitzer on vellum.
4. When the ink is dry, cut the quote apart and run the vellum through a Xyron machine; add to card.

Modern Woman

Janet Klein

MATERIALS

Rubber Stamps: Modern Woman by Janet Klein for Stampotique Originals

Dye Inkpads: Archival Jet Black

Papers: Cardstock; Bond Paper

Pastels/Chalks: Various Chalks

Colored Pencils: Prismacolor

Other: Aqua Eyelets; Transparency

Tools: Sponge; Eyelet Setter; 1/16" Hole Punch; Pencil Blender

INSTRUCTIONS

1. Stamp image on ATC, then stamp on bond paper. Stamp again on scrap paper to make a mask, cut out mask.
2. Color background with pencils, blending colors with blender pencil.
3. Cover colored image with mask; apply layers of chalk. Scribble loose lines of pencil over the chalk.
4. Copy image onto transparency. Align transparency so it fits exactly over ATC stamped image. Trim to fit.
5. Apply adhesive to the black areas of the image on the card, align the transparency, then press it into the glue.
6. Punch holes and attach eyelets.

Maytime Blossom

Janet Klein

MATERIALS

Rubber Stamps: Jill Penny for Stampotique Originals

Dye Inkpads: Ancient Page Plum Wine

Papers: White and Orange Cardstock; Patterned Papers

Paints: Gouache; Watercolors

Colored Pencils: Prismacolor Orange and Metallic Gold

Markers/Pens: PITT Artist Pen

Other: Joss Paper; Purple Eyelets; Number 4 by 7gypsies; Paint Chip

Tools: Eyelet Setter; 1/16" Hole Punch; Small Tip Ninji Brush

INSTRUCTIONS

1. Stamp image on cardstock. Paint stamped image with gouache.
2. Crop and mount paint chip to cardstock. Cut out image and adhere to paint chip.
3. Use PITT pen and colored pencil to add accent with a lined border. Cut out and add number 4.
4. Glue joss paper and patterned paper to card in a pattern to reveal orange ATC background as shown.
5. Angle paint chip card on ATC. Hole punch in corners and add eyelets. Accent edges with pencil.

Charmant

Deb Lewis

MATERIALS

Rubber Stamps: Script by Rubber Baby Buggy Bumpers

Dye Inkpads: Archival Sepia

Papers: Cardstock; Decorative Tissue Paper; Vintage Text Pages

Other: Transparency; Vintage Photograph; Gesso

INSTRUCTIONS

1. Create layers on cardstock by gluing down sheer layers of tissue and text.
2. Attach transparency and vintage photograph; overstamp with script in sepia ink.
3. Paint with gesso, adhere computer-generated word; ink edges with sepia.

Bumble Bee
Christy Hawkins

MATERIALS:
Rubber Stamps: Bee by Magenta
Dye Inkpads: StazOn Jet Black
Papers: Cardstock; Patterned Paper by Provo Craft
Markers/Pens: Summer Sun Zig Scroll and Brush Pen by EK Success; Clear Glaze Pen by Sakura of America
Other: Dymo Label Maker; Flower

INSTRUCTIONS
1. Stamp bee image on ATC; color with pen, add shine with glaze pen.
2. Tear strips of patterned paper and attach to card, add flower.
3. Make title with label maker and attach to finish.

Observation
Christy Hawkins

MATERIALS
Rubber Stamps: Dragonfly by Penny Black; Species No. 1 by Catslife Press; Observation by Postmodern Design; Words "Odonata" and "silvery, lace-like…" by Stampers Anonymous
Dye Inkpads: StazOn Jet Black
and Forest Green
Papers: Cardstock; Vellum; Patterned Paper by Bo Bunny Press
Other: Eyelet; Playing Card; Perfect Pearls and Perfect Medium by Ranger Industries
Tools: Circle Punch; Eyelet Setter

INSTRUCTIONS
1. Stamp dragonfly image on patterned paper with Perfect Medium, dust with Perfect Pearls.
2. Stamp dragonfly image in black on clear vellum; cut out wings and adhere to background as shown.
3. Stamp "species no. 1" in green on pale yellow cardstock; cut out with circle punch, attach with eyelet.

ATC Collection
Christy Hawkins

MATERIALS
Rubber Stamps: Bugs by Stampa Rosa
Dye Inkpads: Memories Black
Papers: White and Pale Yellow Cardstock
Colored Pencils: Prismacolor
Markers/Pens: Black Zig Scroll and Brush Pen by EK Success
Other: Foam Mounting Squares
Tools: Corner Rounder; Paper Trimmer

INSTRUCTIONS
1. Round corners of ATC and edge with pen.
2. Stamp portion of stamp on cardstock twice. Trim base image to fit on ATC.
3. Color the base image with colored pencils on one image, color just the bugs on the other image.
4. Cut out bugs, mount on base image, mat card to finish.

Fly
Christy Hawkins

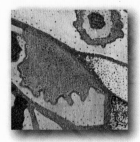

MATERIALS
Rubber Stamps: Wings by Stamp Oasis; Butterflies by All Night Media/Plaid
Dye Inkpads: StazOn Forest Green and Jet Black
Papers: White, Black and Green Cardstock
Paints: Twinkling H2O's
Markers/Pens: Gold Leafing Pen by Krylon
Other: Decorative Punch; Bradletz Letter Brads by Provo Craft
Tools: Corner Rounder; Watercolor Brush

INSTRUCTIONS
1. Stamp images, paint with Twinkling H2O's.
2. Use decorative punch as shown, round corners of image and adhere to ATC.
3. Edge card with gold pen; add letter brads to spell "fly".

BUMBLE BEE

Observation

SILVERY, LACE-LIKE WINGS, PRESENT AT ADULT STAGE

ODONATA

species no. 1

FLY

Believe

Roben-Marie Smith

MATERIALS

Rubber Stamps: Believe by Paperbag Studios; Checker by Stampers Anonymous

Dye Inkpads: StazOn Jet Black

Papers: Butterfly Paper by Autumn Leaves

Markers/Pens: Black Staedtler Triplus Fineliner

Other: Vintage Image from Collage Sheet by Paperbag Studios; Border Sticker by K&Company; Black Mini Brads by Making Memories; Ribbon; Playing Card

Tools: $^1/_{16}$" Hole Punch

INSTRUCTIONS

1. Stamp word on patterned paper as shown, outline butterfly with pen.
2. Stamp portions of checked image randomly, add girl image.
3. Attach ribbon with brads as shown to finish.

X-Ray LOVE

Amy Wellenstein

MATERIALS

Rubber Stamps: Spiraling Out of Control by Stampotique Originals; X-Ray by Fusion Art Stamps; Love by Limited Edition

Pigment Inkpads: VersaMark WaterMark; VersaFine Onyx Black

Papers: Red and White Cardstock

Pastels/Chalks: Various Chalks

Other: Post-it Note

Tools: Heart Punch

INSTRUCTIONS

1. Stamp x-ray image in black ink on white cardstock; stamp again on Post-it, cut out to make a mask.
2. Mask the image and overstamp the spiral background in VersaMark WaterMark. Wait two minutes.
3. With the mask still in place, color background with chalk.
4. Stamp word "love" in black ink, punch heart from red cardstock and adhere as shown.

Cutie Pie

Amy Wellenstein

MATERIALS

Rubber Stamps: Two Cuties Film Strip and Cutie Pie by Catslife Press; "C" from Alphabet Set by Ephemera Design Studio; Dots by B Line Designs

Pigment Inkpads: VersaFine Onyx Black

Dye Inkpads: Adirondack Red Pepper

Papers: Key Lime Pie Paper from Lollipop Shoppe by BasicGrey; White Cardstock

Other: Long Pentagon B Die by Provo Craft

Tools: Circle Punch; Rectangle Punch; Sizzix Die-Cutter

INSTRUCTIONS

1. Stamp background on ATC. Stamp girl image and adhere.
2. Use Sizzix machine and die to cut a small house shape from patterned paper. Cut a small window in the center.
3. Stamp words "cutie pie" and the letter "C", punch out letter and cut out words. Adhere as shown.

Bourbon Street

Roben-Marie Smith

MATERIALS

Rubber Stamps: Bourbon Street by Paperbag Studios

Dye Inkpads: VersaFine Onyx Black

Papers: Autumn Leaves

Other: Metal Arts Sign Language Circle by K&Company; Square Buttons by Making Memories; Playing Card

INSTRUCTIONS

1. Cover a playing card with patterned paper and trim to size.
2. Stamp Bourbon Street in black ink on card front.
3. Adhere button and metal sign language circle to card as shown.

INSTRUCTIONS

1. Adhere patterned paper to card, layer seed packet as shown.
2. Ink word image with coffee ink, color over word "everything", flower and leaves with markers as shown. Attach to card with staples.
3. Punch holes for "grow" brad. Rub VersaMark WaterMark inkpad across entire card front. Sprinkle embossing powder over card and heat set. Repeat until there is a thick layer built up. Put card in freezer for a few minutes, then crack the embossed area as shown.
4. Stamp "friend" onto scrap of white cardstock; trim and adhere to ATC.
5. Attach "grow" brad, add blossom to finish.

Bloom & Grow

Kelly Lunceford

MATERIALS

Rubber Stamps: You Make Everything Bloom by BasicGrey; Antique Lowercase Alphabet by PSX

Pigment Inkpads: Coffee Bean by Inkadinkado; VersaMark WaterMark

Papers: Marcella by K&Company

Markers/Pens: Rubber Stamp Markers by All Night Media/Plaid

Other: Grow Word Brad by K&Company; Blossom by Making Memories; Brad; Staples; Seed Packet; Clear Embossing Powder

Tools: $1/16$" Hole Punch; Heat Tool

Sing, Laugh, Dance

Wendy Sullivan

MATERIALS

Rubber Stamps: Woman by JudiKins; Flower by Hero Arts; Words by All Night Media/Plaid; Flower Cluster by Rubber Stamp Tapestry; Tiny Dots by JRL Design Co.

Pigment Inkpads: VersaMagic Tea Leaves, Thatched Straw and Turquoise Gem

Dye Inkpads: Brilliance Graphite Black

Papers: Olive, Pink and White Cardstock

Other: Cotton Twill Tape; Sequins; Gel Medium by Golden

INSTRUCTIONS

1. Create ATC using two different colors of cardstock; stamp woman image as shown. Stamp pattern on dress.
2. Stamp flowers; attach sequins to centers of flowers.

Grace and Serenity
Wendy Sullivan

MATERIALS

Rubber Stamps: Fish by Fred B. Mullet; Words by Leave Memories; Venus by Appalachian Art Stamps; Bubbles by Rubber Stamps of America

Pigment Inkpads: VersaMagic Cloud White and Brilliance Pearlescent Yellow; Fresco

Sicilian Spice

Dye Inkpads: Brilliance Black; Archival Coffee

Papers: Teal and Ivory Cardstock

Paints: Autumn Skies, Playful Peony, Gold Dust, Sunflower and Fern Twinkling H2O's

Other: Crystal Lacquer

Tools: Heat Tool; Paintbrush

INSTRUCTIONS:

1. Cut teal cardstock ATC size, cut ivory slightly smaller. Stipple inks onto ivory panel.
2. Stamp Venus, heat set. Cut out image, color; trim to fit.
3. Stamp fish and bubbles, heat set. Paint fish and bubbles. Adhere Venus image to card.

Butterfly Kisses
Wendy Sullivan

MATERIALS

Rubber Stamps: Bees by Anita's Art Stamps; Cherub Babies by Appalachian Art Stamps; Flowers by Meer Image; Words by Rubbermoon

Pigment Inkpads: VersaMagic Thatched Straw and Pink Grapefruit

Dye Inkpads: Brilliance

Graohite Black; Archival Coffee; Adirondack Meadow

Papers: Ivory and Cranberry Cardstock

Paints: Sunburst, Playful Peony, Rich Cobalt and Iridescent Violet Twinkling H2O's

Other: Crystal Lacquer

Tools: Heat Tool; Small Watercolor Brush

INSTRUCTIONS

1. Layer ivory and cranberry cardstocks for ATC base.
2. Stipple Meadow, Thatched Straw and Pink Grapefruit onto ATC.
3. Stamp Cherub Babies in black on ivory cardstock; heat set, cut out cherubs image and adhere to card.
4. Stamp bees and flowers; heat set, paint with Twinkling H2O's. Stamp words in black.

Balance & Strength
Wendy Sullivan

MATERIALS

Rubber Stamps: Girl by Acey Deucy; Luna Moth by Meer Image; Words by Leave Memories

Pigment Inkpads: VersaFine White and Blue; Brilliance Pearlescent Yellow

Dye Inkpads: Archival Jet Black and Coffee

Papers: Cardstock

Paints: Gold Dust, Rich Cobalt and Garnet Twinkling H2O's

Tools: Heat Tool; Small Watercolor Brush

INSTRUCTIONS

1. Stamp and cut out all uncolored images on ivory cardstock.
2. Stipple inks for a soft background color.
3. Paint as shown.
4. Layer onto colored cardstock.

Secrets
Wendy Sullivan

MATERIALS

Rubber Stamps: Egg by Tin Can Man/Stampa Rosa; Secrets by Treasure Cay; Promise by Leave Memories; Frame by Stampers Anonymous

Dye Inkpads: Brilliance Graphite Black; Archival Coffee

Paints: Autumn Skies, Red

Poppy, Gold Dust and Cranberry Twinkling H2O's

Papers: Ochre and Ivory Cardstock

Pastels/Chalks: Yellow, Light Blue and Light Aqua Chalks

Other: Mica by USArtQuest

Tools: Heat Tool; Brush

INSTRUCTIONS

1. Cut ochre and ivory cardstock; layer.
2. Stamp eggs on ivory panel, color with chalks. Adhere to ATC base.
3. Stamp frame and word secrets on ivory cardstock, heat set.
4. Tear and cut frame to fit; paint.
5. Adhere mica to back of frame opening, glue frame to ATC. Tear around word secrets, age and adhere.

grace

SERENITY

balance

strength

butterfly kisses

promise

secrets

Style
Christy Hawkins

MATERIALS

Rubber Stamps: Dress on Hanger by Little Lace Lady; Wilde by B Line Designs

Dye Inkpads: StazOn Jet Black

Papers: Fleur de Lis by Creative Imaginations; Black Swirl Print by Scrapbook Wizard; Vellum

Other: Photo Corners; Tulle; Hot Pink Glitter; Cherry Ice and Crystal Ice Stickles by Ranger

INSTRUCTIONS

1. Stamp image on black swirl print, cut out, add tulle.
2. Stamp quote on vellum, cut out, adhere to card.
3. Add photo corners, glitter and Stickles to finish.

Details
Christy Hawkins

MATERIALS

Rubber Stamps: Purses from Accessories by Stampington & Company; "Details" Unmounted Stamp

Pigment Inkpads: Brilliance Galaxy Gold

Dye Inkpads: StazOn Jet Black

Papers: Fleur de Lis Print by Creative Imaginations; White Cardstock

Markers/Pens: Aubergine and English Lavender Zig Scroll and Brush Pens by EK Success

Other: Pink Brads; Gold Fiber; Glass Beads by Darice; Magic Mesh; Photo Corners; Pink Ice Stickles by Ranger

Tools: Heat Tool

INSTRUCTIONS

1. Adhere patterned paper for background.
2. Stamp purses and cut out. Cover with beads, trim with fibers. Attach with brads.
3. Stamp word "Details", add Magic Mesh along side of card and mount photo corners to finish.

Relic
Christy Hawkins

MATERIALS

Rubber Stamps: Corset, Tape Measure and Unmounted Stamps by Oxford Impressions; Relic by Postmodern Design

Dye Inkpads: StazOn Jet Black

Papers: Fleur de Lis by Creative Imaginations; Bisque Cardstock by Bazzill Basics

Markers/Pens: English Lavender, Sagebrush and Rose Zig Scroll and Brush Pens by EK Success

Other: Metal Flower and Lavender Brad by American Tag; Pink Ice Stickles by Ranger; Photo Corners; Snaps

INSTRUCTIONS

1. Adhere patterned paper to ATC as shown, stamp corset on cardstock, color, cut out and adhere to card.
2. Stamp snaps, add metal flower to snap with brad, add photo corners.

Other: Photo Corners; Snow-Tex by Deco Art; Feather; Jewel Crystal Ice and Lime Green Ice Stickles from by Ranger

Tools: Square Punch

INSTRUCTIONS

1. Stamp quote on patterned paper. Stamp woman images, color with pens and punch out.
2. Mount images on cardstock and adhere to card.
3. Add feather and jewel, adhere photo corners to finish.

Accessorize
Christy Hawkins

MATERIALS

Rubber Stamps: Fancy Hats by Hero Arts; Olympia Dukakis Quote by Ann-ticipations

Dye Inkpads: StazOn Jet Black

Papers: Fleur de Lis by Creative Imaginations; Bisque and Black Cardstock by Bassill Basics

Markers/Pens: Sagebrush, English Lavender, Aubergine, Summer Sun, Rose, Pure Blue, Coffee and Wheat Zig Scroll and Brush Pens by EK Success

Mom was a Beauty

Janet Klein

MATERIALS

Rubber Stamps: Beach Beauty and Circle Border by Stampotique Originals

Pigment Inkpads: VersaColor Split Pea

Dye Inkpads: Ancient Page Lapis

Papers: 7gypsies; White Cardstock; Book Page; Light Brown Paper

Paints: Diluted White Acrylic

Pastels/Chalks: Lapis, Aqua and White Neoart Wax Pastels by Caran d'Ache

Colored Pencils: Prismacolor Violet, White, Indigo, Aqua and White

Other: Graphite Pencil; Two Aqua Eyelets; Organza Ribbon

Tools: Small Flat Paintbrush; $^1/_{16}$" Eyelets; Eyelet Setter; Heat Tool

INSTRUCTIONS

1. Whitewash book page; let dry, trim and adhere to white cardstock.
2. Apply lapis and aqua pastels to card. Paint over with damp brush to create color wash. Let dry.
3. Stamp Beach Beauty in lapis, color with pencils, cut out.
4. Stamp Circle Border in Split Pea. Dry with heat tool.
5. Type "Beauty" on computer; print on light brown paper and glue in place along with scraps of page.
6. Accent edges with wax pastels; add tape measure, eyelets and ribbon.

Imagine Yourself Here

Amy Wellenstein

MATERIALS

Rubber Stamps: Woman from Buttons by PaperArtsy; Imagine Yourself Here by Catslife Press; Buttons by Paperbag Studios; Texture Tile by Stampendous; Hook and Eye Border by Stampotique Originals

Pigment Inkpads: VersaMark WaterMark; VersaFine Onyx Black; ColorBox Chestnut Roan

Papers: White Cardstock

Pastels/Chalks: Various Chalks

Other: Post-it Note

INSTRUCTIONS

1. Stamp women on white cardstock in black ink. Color the image with chalks.
2. Stamp woman again and cut out to mask the image; overstamp tile background repeatedly in VersaMark WaterMark. Wait two minutes.
3. Color the background with black and red chalks.
4. Stamp Buttons and Imagine Yourself Here in black ink. Stamp Hook and Eye Border in Chestnut Roan ink.

Seeing Through

Roben-Marie Smith

MATERIALS

Rubber Stamps: Seeing by Paperbag Studios

Dye Inkpads: StazOn Jet Black

Papers: Robin's Egg Classic Circles and Kids Stripes by Daisy D's; Lollipop by BasicGrey

Other: Playing Card; Eyelets by Making Memories; Green Checked Ribbon

Tools: Eyelet Setter; $^1/_{16}$" Hole Punch

INSTRUCTIONS

1. Stamp Seeing onto Lollipop paper in black ink and cut out one window and quote, adhere.
2. Punch holes into top right and left corners of card; set eyelets into holes, add ribbon.

Wings to Fly

Jill Haglund

MATERIALS

Rubber Stamps: Butterfly Girl by Claudine Hellmuth

Dye Inkpads: Memories Black

Paper: Purple Cardstock

Other: Tags; Bubble Heart; Instant Coffee

INSTRUCTIONS

1. Coffee-dye tag with string using hot water and concentrated instant coffee. Iron dry and flat.
2. Stamp image in black and adhere heart.
3. Layer onto purple cardstock cut ATC size as shown.

Art Brushes

Janet Klein

MATERIALS

Rubber Stamps: Tile Wall by Paperbag Studios; Sable and Fanny Brush Images by Janet Klein for Stampotique Originals

Pigment Inkpads: VersaMark WaterMark

Dye Inkpads: Archival Jet Black

Papers: White Cardstock

Paints: Light Aqua and Hot Pink Acrylic

Pastels/Chalks: Fuchsia Chalk

Colored Pencils: Prismacolor

Other: Fiber; Trim; Post-it Note

Tools: Cosmetic Sponge; Small Tip Brush; Heat Tool

INSTRUCTIONS

1. Stamp brush images in black ink on white cardstock; stamp image again on post-it note and cut out to create mask.
2. Cover brush images with masks, stamp tile wall image in VersaMark WaterMark, heat set.
3. With masks in place, apply fuchsia chalk with sponge.
4. Enhance images with pencils and acrylics. Run fuchsia pencil along edge of card. Attach fiber trim along back edge.

Dream

Deanna Furey

MATERIALS

Rubber Stamps: Bee by Anna Griffin; Butterfly by JudiKins; Leaf by Inkadinkado; Flower by Hero Arts; Dot Stamp by Treasure Cay; Shadow Oval and Square by Hero Arts; Dream by EK Success.

Pigment Inkpads: VersaMagic Aegean Blue and Aloe Vera; Brilliance Galaxy Gold and Cosmic Copper

Dye Inkpads: Archival Coffee, Sepia and Library Green

Papers: Green and Cream Cardstock

Other: Crystal Glitter by Stampendous

INSTRUCTIONS

1. Stamp cardstock background as shown. On a separate piece of cardstock stamp word "dream", butterfly and leaf, cut out.
2. Stamp flower image twice more and cut out. Glue flowers together as shown.
3. Attach the word "dream", butterfly and leaf with foam tape; apply glitter to wings and petals. Layer onto cardstock.

Serendipity

(W)hole Numbers

Janet Klein

MATERIALS

Rubber Stamps: Numbers by Paperbag Studios

Pigment Inkpads: VersaColor Split Pea

Dye Inkpads: Ancient Page Deep Harbor

Papers: Cardstock

Paints: Yellow, Teal and Green Twinkling H20's

Pastels/Chalks: Neoart Wax Pastels by Caran d'Ache

Colored Pencils: Prismacolor Orange, Yellow, White and Teal; Teal, Lime and Yellow Watercolor Pencils

Markers/Pens: PITT Artist Pen; White Souffle Gel Pen by Sakura of America; Gold Metallic Paint Pen

Tools: 1/16" Hole Punch; Corner Rounder

INSTRUCTIONS

1. Color sides of card with teal; bring lime, then yellow, to the center. Blend colors with a damp brush, accent with Twinkling H20's.
2. Stamp image in dye ink. Clean stamp and stamp same image with pigment ink on black scrap.
3. Trim black piece to overlap portion of stamped image on card.
4. Accent numbers with pencils, round corners and edge with paint pen to finish.

Play All Day

Jill Haglund

MATERIALS

Rubber Stamps: Clown, Tickets and Wings by Invoke Arts; Small Starburst by PSX

Pigment Inkpads: VersaFine Onyx Black; ColorBox Cat's Eye Lavender and Peach Pastel

Papers: Red, Orange and White Cardstock

Colored Pencils: Prismacolor

Other: Playing Card

Tools: Pigment Ink Sponge Applicator by Clearsnap

INSTRUCTIONS

1. Apply ink to ATC using sponge applicator.
2. Stamp tickets as shown, cut out and adhere. Stamp clown on ATC.
3. Stamp wings onto cardstock, cut out and place behind clown.
4. Stamp hat; color and cut out, adhere to clown. Stamp starburst as shown.

Red Family Memories Album

Judith Godwin

MATERIALS

Rubber Stamps: Postcard Collage by Hampton Art Stamps; Face by River City Rubberworks; A Fun Time by Rubbermoon; Family and Memories (source unknown)

Dye Inkpads: Archival Jet Black

Papers: Red and Black Cardstock; Black and White Text Weight Paper; Red Patterned Paper; Faces Patterned Paper

Colored Pencils: Faber-Castell Flesh, Tan and Red

Other: Transparency; Thick Cardstock or Thin Chipboard

Tools: 1" and 5/8" Square Punch; Stapler

INSTRUCTIONS

1. Stamp postcard collage background with black ink on red cardstock.
2. Stamp A Fun Time with black ink on red cardstock; trim closely and adhere.
3. Make a book by taping together two pieces of 1 1/2 " x 2" pieces chipboard at the spine. Punch hole in front cover with 5/8" punch. Cover and adhere front and back of book with patterned paper. (To cover front of booklet cut an X in the red background paper, wrap to the inside; glue in place). Tape cut and trimmed piece of transparency over punched square.
4. Stamp face image in black ink on white cardstock and color tape face to window inside of book.
5. Stamp Family and Memories in black ink on front cover under window.

Dream Ticket

Roben-Marie Smith

MATERIALS

Rubber Stamps: Numbers Stamp by Postmodern Design

Dye Inkpads: StazOn Jet Black

Papers: Flare by Rusty Pickle

Paints: White Acrylic by Delta; Oil Pastels by Loew Cornell; White Gesso by Golden

Other: Freezer Paper; Vintage Image by Paperbag Studios; Spray Sealant by Krylon; Playing Card

Tools: Heat Tool

INSTRUCTIONS

1. Paint one side of card with white gesso and heat set.
2. In a grid format, rub yellow and then green oil pastels onto card. Gently rub with finger.
3. Rub red and blue oil pastels into card with finger.
4. Using a black pastel, mark lines to highlight different colors. Spray seal with Krylon sealer. Squeeze small drops of white acrylic paint onto freezer paper in random spots. Close the paper and gently smooth. Open and place the trading card face down onto small areas of paint. Lift and heat set.
5. Stamp image on side of card. Adhere small piece of patterned paper.
6. Cut out vintage girl image from collage sheet.
7. Cut out ticket from patterned paper; adhere to girl image, attach to card.
8. Computer-generate word "dream" and add to card to finish.

New York
Dawn Binyon

MATERIALS

Rubber Stamps: New York Collage by PSX; Mini Statue of Liberty by A Country Welcome

Dye Inkpads: StazOn Jet Black

Markers/Pens: Red Marvy Matchable Pen

Papers: Glossy Cardstock; Mulberry Paper

INSTRUCTIONS

1. Stamp New York Collage on ATC; edge with red pen.
2. Stamp Mini Statue of Liberty on mulberry paper and attach.

No. 7821
Roben-Marie Smith

MATERIALS

Rubber Stamps: Sentiments by Paperbag Studios

Dye Inkpads: VersaFine Onyx Black

Papers: Birthday Plaid Classic Pink by Daisy D's; Pink Stripe by Rusty Pickle

Other: Ribbon; Eyelet Brad

Tools: 1/16" Hole Punch

INSTRUCTIONS

1. Cover card with plaid patterned paper, trim to size.
2. Stamp Sentiments on striped paper and trim, adhere to card.
3. Punch hole, add brad and tie ribbon.

Black & White Sun Ornament
Dawn Binyon

MATERIALS

Rubber Stamps: Printed Circle with Face by Stampers Anonymous; Swirls and Curls by Stampabilities

Inkpads: StazOn Jet Black

Papers: Glossy Cardstock

Markers/Pens: Silver Leafing Pen by Krylon

INSTRUCTIONS

1. Stamp background swirl image on ATC.
2. Stamp focal image four times, cut out each image. Layer with pop dots, cut edges to fit ATC.
3. Edge with leafing pen and attach piece to swirl background with pop dots.

Threads of Gold
Beautiful & Strong

Treasure Each Day
Roben-Marie Smith

MATERIALS

Rubber Stamps: Silences and Hole Punched by Paperbag Studios

Dye Inkpads: StazOn Jet Black

Papers: Grey Ochre by BasicGrey

Other: Rub-On Words by Making Memories; Buttons; Prescription; Playing Card

INSTRUCTIONS

1. Adhere patterned paper to ATC-sized cardstock.
2. Stamp focal image tear and adhere.
3. Stamp Hole Punched image on side and bottom.
4. Apply rub-on words; glue buttons.

Something Special
Roben-Marie Smith

MATERIALS

Rubber Stamps: Block Trio and Something Special by Paperbag Studios

Dye Inkpads: VersaFine Onyx Black

Papers: Fiore Classic Blue, Overalls Classic Stripe and Robin's Egg Classic Circles by Daisy D's

Other: Dictionary Paper; Stitch Bubble Strip by K&Company

Tools: Daisy Punch

INSTRUCTIONS

1. Cover card with patterned paper, trim. Stamp Block Trio; cut out two of the blocks, adhere.
2. Punch through patterned paper and dictionary paper. Glue to top of each square on card.
3. Stamp Something Special, adhere bubble strip to edges of card.

To Serve
Roben-Marie Smith

MATERIALS

Rubber Stamps: Flower Bud and Lace by Paperbag Studios

Dye Inkpads: VersaFine Onyx Black

Papers: Newsletter-S by Basic Grey; Robin's Egg Classic Stripe by Daisy D's

Other: Quote Unquote Stickers by Autumn Leaves

INSTRUCTIONS

1. Cover ATC with patterned paper, stamp Lace onto card as shown.

2. Stamp Flower Bud, cut out and adhere to card with pop dot.
3. Adhere quote to card to finish.

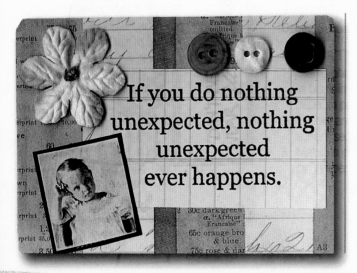

Unexpected
Roben-Marie Smith

MATERIALS

Rubber Stamps: Unexpected by Paperbag Studios

Dye Inkpads: StazOn Jet Black

Papers: Striped Paper by FoofaLa; Ledger Bookkeeper by Making Memories

Other: Flower by Prima Marketing; Buttons; Vintage Photo

INSTRUCTIONS

1. Adhere striped paper to card.
2. Stamp Unexpected on ledger paper, cut out and adhere.
3. Adhere layered vintage image with glue stick. Attach buttons and flower with glue dots.

Giggle
Roben-Marie Smith

MATERIALS

Rubber Stamps: Hole Punched and Giggle by Paperbag Studios
Dye Inkpads: StazOn Jet Black
Papers: White Wash Hydrangea by Sonburn, LLC; Black by 7gypsies
Other: Vintage Photo; Old Prescription Label; Chipboard Letter by Li'l Davis Designs
Tools: Flower Punch; Sewing Machine

INSTRUCTIONS

1. Stamp Hole Punched images several times on right edge of card.
2. Tear and adhere a scrap of old prescription label to the left edge of card.
3. Using flower punch, create two flowers with the black paper and glue to card.
4. Layer vintage photos as shown and adhere to card

Tres Amigas
Janet Klein

MATERIALS

Rubber Stamps: Little Friends, Tiny, Lissi and Number Stamp from Random Acts Alphabet Set by Janet Klein for Stampotique Originals
Pigment Inkpads: VersaMagic Pink Petunia
Dye Inkpads: Adirondack Black
Papers: Cardstock; Newsprint
Paints: Light Pink and Magenta Acrylic
Colored Pencils: Prismacolor Pinks, Green and White
Other: Pink Eyelet and Embroidery Floss; Walnut Spray Ink; White Gesso; Funquins Razzle by Willow Bead
Tools: Cosmetic Sponge; Sponge Brush; Sewing Machine; Eyelet Setter; Hole Punches

INSTRUCTIONS

1. Apply thinned gesso with sponge brush to newspaper. Let dry. Adhere to ATC-sized cardstock.
2. Spray with walnut ink; wipe with sponge, let dry.
3. Stamp Lissi on card in black ink. Stamp Little Friends and Tiny to scrap cardstock. Trim to make small tag, punch hole in top of tag.
4. Stamp No. 3 in pink to right of Lissi image, scribble behind image and create a border in assorted colors as shown.
5. Use sewing machine to pierce holes around edge of card.
6. Computer-generate "tres amigas", cut out and adhere.
7. Use fingertip to paint a random border, attach eyelet in upper left corner. Attach tag with pink embroidery floss.

Retro
Amy Wellenstein

MATERIALS

Rubber Stamps: Modern Woman, Snaps and Scraffitti Letters by Stampotique Originals; Dots by Hot Potatoes; Number Stamp by Limited Edition
Pigment Inkpads: VersaFine Onyx Black and Green; VersaMark WaterMark
Papers: White Cardstock
Pastels/Chalks: Various Chalks
Other: Post-it Note
Tools: Sponge

INSTRUCTIONS

1. Stamp Modern Woman on white cardstock; stamp again on a Post-it Note, cut out both.
2. Mask over ATC image and stamp dots for background in VersaMark WaterMark. Let dry for two minutes.
3. With mask in place, rub green, yellow and blue shades of chalk over dot images with sponge.
4. Lift mask and stamp "RETRO" and snap border in black; stamp "No. 074819" on right in green. Color woman with chalk.

I Never Travel...
Ginny Carter Smallenberg

MATERIALS

Rubber Stamps: Two-Faced, Newspaper Scraps, Binding Edge and I Never Travel by Stampers Anonymous

Dye Inkpads: StazOn Black, Mustard, Royal Purple and Blazing Red

Papers: MatteKote by JudiKins; Cardstock

Markers/Pens: PITT Artist Pen
Other: Black Cording
Tools: Sponge

INSTRUCTIONS

1. Stamp images on MatteKote paper, sponge in colors from inkpads.
2. Color with PITT pens; trim and adhere to cardstock base, add binding edge and image to finish.

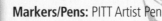

Looking Out
Ginny Carter Smallenburg

MATERIALS

Rubber Stamps: Wistful Woman, Glory of Art and Leaf Border #1 by Stampers Anonymous

Dye Inkpads: Memories Black and Cherry Red

Papers: Yellow and Red Cardstock

Markers/Pens: Gold Galaxy Marker by American Crafts

INSTRUCTIONS

1. Stamp Glory of Art on yellow cardstock, stamp leaf border on red cardstock, cut and adhere.
2. Stamp Wistful Woman image, trim and adhere.
3. Highlight leaf border with pen.

Memories
Ginny Carter Smallenburg

MATERIALS

Rubber Stamps: Text by Stampers Anonymous

Dye Inkpads: StazOn Jet Black and Mustard

Papers: Black Cardstock; BasicGrey

Markers/Pens: Black Brush Marker by Marvy

Other: Vintage Photo; Photo Corners; Index Card; Stencil

INSTRUCTIONS

1. Tear paper, adhere to side. Cut index card and sew as shown.
2. Adhere vintage photo.
3. Stamp text on scrap paper. Rub with mustard ink.
4. Use "5" stencil to trace letter over stamped text. Cut out and outline with black marker.
5. Assemble all pieces as shown.

Unedited Street Art
Wendy Sullivan

MATERIALS

Rubber Stamps: Art Image by Lost Coast

Dye Inkpads: StazOn Jet Black

Papers: Teal and White Cardstock; Holographic Paper

Other: Bottle Cap; Seed Beads; Star Sequins; Brad; Transparency; Photograph; JudiKins Diamond Glaze

Tools: Round Punch

INSTRUCTIONS:

1. Adhere photograph to card, stamp Art Image on scrap paper, scale down to fit card; print out on transparency.
2. Punch out face portion, glue into bottle cap with Diamond Glaze. Adhere photograph image to card; attach transparency with brad as shown.
3. Stamp domino portion of the Art stamp image onto a scrap of holographic paper, adhere to card with foam tape.
4. When bottle cap is dry, fill with beads and sequins. Punch a piece of acetate, then run a line of diamond glaze around the edge and place on top of bottle cap to dry, attach to card with double-stick tape.

Remember
Annieta Vries

MATERIALS

Rubber Stamps: Lady by The Stampsmith; Background Text by Hero Arts; Old French Writing from Text Remember by Oxford Impressions
Dye Inkpads: Memories Black
Papers: White and Silver Cardstock

Markers/Pens: Black Fine Tip Marker; Silver Leafing Pen by Krylon
Other: Silver Stickers; Black Napkin; Silver Glitter Stick; Spray Adhesive

INSTRUCTIONS

1. Spray-mount a 3/4" strip of one layer of black napkin to left side of ATC-sized white cardstock.
2. Stamp Lady in black on another piece of cardstock. Stamp again; cut out to use as mask. Stamp background text in black; trim and adhere to meet napkin. Edge with marker.
3. Mat onto ATC-sized silver cardstock. Apply silver glitter stick, add star sticker to bottom right.
4. Stamp, cut out edge in silver the "Remember".
5. Adhere to card.

"F" is for Friendship

Wendy Sulllivan

MATERIALS

Rubber Stamps: Friendship by Uptown Rubber Stamps; Woman's Face by Rubbermoon

Dye Inkpads: StazOn Jet Black

Papers: Print Blocks by Design Originals; Teal Cardstock; Mat Board

Pens/Markers: Gold Krylon

Other: Page from an Old Book; Acetate Transparency; Copper Brads; Orange and Brown Pinata Alcohol Inks and Claro Medium by Jaquard

Tools: Ink Spreader for Alcohol Inks by Jaquard; 1/8" Hole Punch

INSTRUCTIONS

1. Cut teal cardstock to ATC size. Cut page from an old book and layer on top as shown.
2. Cut an "F" from the print blocks paper and glue to a piece of mat board; edge the mat board piece with gold pen.
3. Cut a piece of acetate transparency slightly smaller then ATC, stamp woman's face and words with black Stazon on acetate, as shown.
4. Turn transparency and add dots with gold pen. Add a tiny drop of each of the inks; add a drop of Claro medium; mix with ink spreader at bottom. Let dry.
5. Attach transparency to prepared card with copper brads; adhere "F" with tape.

Able to Create

Carolyn Peeler

MATERIALS

Rubber Stamps: Script Background by Penny Black

Pigment Inkpads: VersaMark WaterMark

Papers: Handmade Background Paper

Paints: Red Acrylic

Pastels/Chalks: Pink Chalk

Other: Vintage Photograph; Red Embossing Powder

Tools: Heat Tool

INSTRUCTIONS

1. Cut background paper to ATC size; stamp script in VersaMark WaterMark, sprinkle on embossing powder, heat emboss.
2. Cut out images of girls from a vintage photograph; tint cheeks with chalk and adhere.
3. Computer-generate "able to create" and adhere.
4. Dip toothpick in red paint to add dots to the collars, cuffs and skirt.

Play with Bears

Carolyn Peeler

MATERIALS

Rubber Stamps: Old Label by Anna Griffin for All Night Media/Plaid

Pigment Inkpads: Anna Griffin Green

Dye Inkpads: Adirondack Latte

Papers: White Cardstock; Pink Dot Paper by Anna Griffin

Pastels/Chalks: Pink Chalk

Other: Vintage Photograph; Stickers by Making Memories

INSTRUCTIONS

1. Cut pink dot paper to ATC size; distress with sandpaper, ink edges in brown.
2. Stamp label onto white cardstock with green ink; cut out, ink edges in brown.
3. Cut out little girl from vintage photo; tint cheeks with pink chalk.
4. Glue label and girl image to card; adhere word and letter stickers to label, sew buttons to card as shown.

wild
child

Wild Child

Carlene Federer

MATERIALS

Rubber Stamps: Leopard Print by Stampin' Up!

Pigment Inkpads: ColorBox Orange and Pink

Other: Image by ARTchix Studios; Decorative Tape by Heidi Swapp; Rhinestone; Clear Embossing Powder

Tools: Heat Tool

INSTRUCTIONS

1. Stamp leopard print on ATC; clear emboss and heat set.
2. Adhere image; frame with decorative tape.
3. Computer-generate title; adhere to ATC.
4. Add rhinestone to finish.

Copper Fish

Janet Klein

MATERIALS

Rubber Stamps: Fish by Tin Can Mail/Stamp Rosa

Pigment Inkpads: ColorBox Yellows, Pinks and Corals

Dye Inkpads: Ancient Page Palm

Papers: Cream Cardstock

Markers/Pens: Gold and Copper Metallic Markers; Black PITT Artist Pen

Other: Copper Scrap; Ultra Thick Embossing Enamel by Suze Weinberg; Patina Aging Solution by Modern Masters; Playing Card

Tools: Heat Gun

INSTRUCTIONS

1. Cut small rectangle from copper. Drizzle patina solution on copper, set aside.
2. Randomly stamp card with assorted pigment inks, emboss. Repeat process for thick tile-like surface.
3. Stamp fish in Palm on cream cardstock; cut out, accent details with PITT pen.
4. Glue copper to center of card.

Nostalgia

Judith Godwin

MATERIALS

Rubber Stamps: Mitchell and Roy Russell by B Line Designs

Dye Inkpads: Archival Jet Black

Papers: Beige Cardstock

Other: Walnut Ink; Silver Eyelets; Metal Corners from Lost Art Treasures by American Tag; Vintage Image (50's Girl); Vellum Quote Stacks Transparency by DieCuts with a View

Tools: Eyelet Setter; Hole Punch

INSTRUCTIONS

1. Stamp male images in black ink on cardstock.
2. Add corners to 50's girl image, tape image to card.
3. Punch holes and attach eyelets to vellum and card.

Travel

Judith Godwin

MATERIALS

Rubber Stamps: Sedan and Passengers by B Line Designs; All Occasion by Stamp It Up; Colosseum by All Night Media/Plaid

Dye Inkpads: Archival Black and Blue

Papers: White, Black, Brown and Blue Cardstock; Section of Map

Other: JudiKins Diamond Glaze; Two Plastic Tires from Toy Car

INSTRUCTIONS

1. Cut blue cardstock to ATC size; stamp car in black and cut out.
2. Stamp Colosseum in black on brown paper, cut out and glue as shown; layer torn map.
3. Stamp people on blue cardstock, reduce images on color copier, cut out and place in car windows.
4. Glue car over map, add wheels and the word "TRAVEL".

Love

Amy Wellenstein

MATERIALS

Rubber Stamps: Wings (Plate 4) by PaperArtsy; Love by Limited Edition

Dye Inkpads: StazOn Jet Black; Kaleidacolor Melon Medley

Papers: Glossy White Cardstock

Tools: Soft Rubber Brayers

INSTRUCTIONS

1. Brayer colored dye inkpad onto glossy cardstock. Let dry.
2. Ink a second brayer with black ink.
3. Brayer ink onto the stamps and stamp images as shown.

Surely All This

Amy Wellenstein

MATERIALS

Rubber Stamps: Wings (Plate 3) by PaperArtsy; Surely All This is Not Without Meaning by Leavenworth Jackson; Text by Zettiology

Dye Inkpads: StazOn Jet Black and Blazing Red; Kaleidacolor Desert Heat

Papers: Cardstock

Tools: Soft Rubber Brayers

INSTRUCTIONS

1. Brayer colored dye inkpad onto glossy cardstock. Let dry.
2. Ink a second brayer with black ink.
3. Brayer ink onto the stamps and stamp images as shown.

Fortune Cookie

Carlene Federer

MATERIALS

Rubber Stamps: Lip Stamp by Rubber Stampede

Pigment Inkpads: ColorBox Red

Other: Image by ARTchix Studios; Photo Turn by 7gypsies; Rhinestone; Fortune from Fortune Cookie

INSTRUCTIONS

1. Stamp lip image randomly on ATC.
2. Add ARTchix image, fortune, photo turn and rhinestone.

Sick Parrot Post

Amy Wellenstein

MATERIALS

Rubber Stamps: Wings (Plate 2) by PaperArtsy; Sick Parrot Post by Limited Edition; Bangkok Post by Tin Can Mail/Stampa Rosa

Dye Inkpads: StazOn Jet Black and Blazing Red; Kaleidacolor Caribbean Sea

Papers: Glossy White Cardstock

Tools: Soft Rubber Brayers

INSTRUCTIONS

1. Brayer colored dye inkpad onto glossy cardstock. Let dry.
2. Ink a second brayer with black ink.
3. Brayer ink onto the stamps and stamp images as shown.

Wild Thing Post
Amy Wellenstein

MATERIALS

Rubber Stamps: Eclectic (Plate 2) by PaperArtsy; Antique Border by Stampotique Originals; Alexandrie Post by Tin Can Mail/Stampa Rosa

Dye Inkpads: StazOn Jet Black; Kaleidacolor Creole Spice

Papers: Glossy White Cardstock

Tools: Soft Rubber Brayers

INSTRUCTIONS

1. Brayer colored dye inkpad onto glossy cardstock. Let dry.
2. Ink a second brayer with black ink.
3. Brayer ink onto the stamps and stamp images as shown.

Fly Safely
Amy Wellenstein

MATERIALS

Rubber Stamps: Wings (Plate 3) by PaperArtsy

Dye Inkpads: StazOn Jet Black; Kaleidacolor Blue Breeze

Papers: Glossy White Cardstock

Other: Dymo Label Maker

Tools: Soft Rubber Brayers

INSTRUCTIONS

1. Brayer colored dye inkpad onto glossy cardstock. Let dry.
2. Ink a second brayer with b`lack ink.
3. Brayer ink onto the stamps and stamp images as shown.
4. Add label.

Orange Shrine with Photo
Amy Wellenstein

MATERIALS

Rubber Stamps: Decorative Background by Magenta; Shrine by Stampers Anonymous; Italian Script by Acey Deucy; Number Stamp by Limited Edition

Pigment Inkpads: VersaMark WaterMark; VersaFine Onyx Black

Papers: White, Black and Orange Cardstock

Pastels/Chalks: Various Chalks

Other: Photo

Tools: Xacto Knife

INSTRUCTIONS:

1. Stamp Decorative Background on white cardstock in VersaMark WaterMark ink; let dry, color with pink and yellow chalks.
2. Stamp Shrine in black ink in the center of the chalked panel, stamp "No. 074819" below the shrine image. Trim the window out of the shrine using Xacto knife.
3. Adhere photo to back of stamped panel.
4. Stamp Italian Script repeatedly on orange cardstock in black ink.
5. Layer stamped panels on black cardstock.

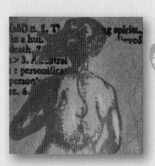

Sand Dollar Woman

Janet Klein

MATERIALS

Rubber Stamps: Rear View Mirror (Woman), Baroque and Spirit Definition by Stampotique Originals

Pigment Inkpads: ColorBox Copper

Dye Inkpads: Archival Sepia and Jet Black

Papers: Cardstock

Colored Pencils: Prismacolor Sepia, Greens and White

Other: Sand Dollar Charm; Copper Grommet; Gold Craft Wire; Glass Bugle Beads; Post-it Notes; Ultra Thick Embossing Enamel by Suze Weinberg

Tools: Cosmetic Sponge; Eyelet Setter; 1/8" Hole Punch; Heat Tool

INSTRUCTIONS

1. Stamp Rear View Mirror on cardstock in sepia ink. Stamp image on Post-it Note and cut out to create mask.
2. Stamp Baroque in sepia ink on scrap cardstock and create a small tag.
3. Stamp edge of card in copper ink, sprinkle with embossing powder; emboss.
4. Use mask to cover figure image and mask embossed border, stamp Spirit Definition in black ink.
5. With masks in place, blend chalks with sponge; remove masks.
6. Use colored pencils to scribble loose lines for background; use white pencil to accent figure.
7. Punch holes along inside of stamped border, string beads on wire and weave through holes.
8. Attach an eyelet to the bottom, layer charm over small tag and secure with wire.

Charmed Garden

Janet Klein

MATERIALS

Rubber Stamps: Planting Stamp by Janet Klein for Stampotique Originals

Pigment Inkpads: ColorBox Bronze

Papers: Scrap of Italian Script Paper; Scrap Mat Board; cardstock

Paints: Twinkling H2O's

Markers/Pens: Black PITT Fine Tip Artist Pen

Other: Gold Micro Beads; Double-Sided Tape; Gold Charm; Ultra Thick Embossing Powder by Suze Weinberg

Tools: Heat Tool

INSTRUCTIONS

1. Apply bronze ink to precut mat board, sprinkle with embossing powder, heat.
2. Apply a second layer and repeat the process; this time stamp into the warm surface.
3. Tape edges of image, sprinkle with gold micro beads.
4. Tear Italian Script paper and layer as shown on ATC.
5. Adhere mat board to layered cardstock.

Abellimento

Janet Klein

MATERIALS

Rubber Stamps: Text Block by Amy Wilson Willenstein for Stampotique Originals; Clown by Invoke Arts

Pigment Inkpads: VersaMark WaterMark; ColorBox Copper and Terra Cotta

Dye Inkpads: Adirondack Sepia

Papers: Cardstock and Specialty Paper

Paints: Watercolors

Markers: Copper by Krylon

Other: Wire; Eyelets; Bead; Gold Embossing Powders; Copper Glitter Pen

Tools: Heat Tool; Eyelet Setter; 1/16" Hole Punch; Small Tip Ninji Water Brush; Sponges

INSTRUCTIONS

1. Touch ATC with green and yellow inkpads here and there for background. Allow to dry. Rub VersaMark WaterMark inkpad lightly on front over inked colors; sprinkle with gold embossing powder, heat set. Trim card with copper Krylon pen.
2. Stamp focal image twice on cardstock in sepia. Stamp image again on red specialty paper. Cut out sepia image. Cut hat from red specialty paper and adhere as shown. Touch collar and eyebrows with glitter pen. Paint cheeks with watercolor using Ninji Brush.
3. Stamp text block on a scrap of cardstock in Sepia. Use Terra Cotta ink to rub cardstock front and edges. Punch holes and set eyelets in four corners, thread wires through eyelets and twist.
4. Secure panel by adding glue and taping all wires to back of ATC. Adhere clown with foam tape.
5. Punch small hole in bottom center of ATC, add bead with wire.

Rose Goddess

Corrine Byers

MATERIALS

Rubber Stamps: Face Rose Stamp by Articus Studio

Dye Inkpads: StazOn Black; Summer Sun by Stampin' Up!

Colored Pencils: Prismacolor Green and Rose

Markers/Pens: Rose Art Markers

Other: Stampboard; Krylon Kamar Varnish; Tim Holtz "Light Words" Distressables Cutable Strips by Design Originals

Tools: Dual-Tipped ColorBox Stylus

INSTRUCTIONS

1. Use stylus to apply color to cut stampboard, starting with lighter color.
2. Stamp images; color as shown with pencils and markers.
3. Add word strip.

Adventure

Kelly Lunceford

MATERIALS

Rubber Stamps: Express It and Date Stamp by Making Memories; The Isle of Pelicos Stamp Set by Nick Bantock

Pigment Inkpads: VersaMagic Tea Leaves; Anna Griffin Cream

Dye Inkpads: StazOn Timber Brown and Olive Green; Inkstone Sea by Rubber Stampede

Papers: Brown and Ivory Cardstock

Other: Bookplate with Brads and Ribbon Words by Making Memories; Ribbon

Tools: Sewing Machine; 1/16" Hole Punch

INSTRUCTIONS

1. Stamp lizard and compass images in cream ink on brown cardstock; stamp "escape" in green.
2. Adhere "explore" ribbon word to a small scrap of ivory cardstock.
3. Stamp "adventure" over the top in brown, attach to card front and add bookplate with brads.
4. Stamp airmail in green and layer postmark image stamped in brown, mat onto ivory cardstock. Adhere to card front.
5. Stamp destination and date in Inkstone Sea ink onto small scraps.
6. Wrap around the card and stitch "destination" as shown with brown thread.

Find Peace Within

Cris Cunningham

MATERIALS

Rubber Stamps: Pixie Sentiments by PSX; Crackle Background by The Moon Rose Art Stamps

Dye Inkpads: Archival Jet Black and Sepia

Papers: Ivory Cardstock; Old World Texture by DieCuts With A View

Markers/Pens: Copper Leafing Pen by Krylon

Other: Female Image; Gold Scrap Border by ARTchix Studio

Tools: Small Sponge

INSTRUCTIONS

1. Stamp background in sepia on white cardstock.
2. Adhere torn paper and female image, stamp "find peace within" in black, cut out and adhere.
3. Sponge edges with sepia ink, edge with leafing pen.
4. Attach gold scrap border to top of card.

One Boy
Janet Klein

MATERIALS
Rubber Stamps: Boy Image by PaperArtsy; No. 1 by Stampotique Originals

Pigment Inkpads: Brilliance Peacock

Dye Inkpads: Archival Library Green

Papers: White Cardstock

Colored Pencils: Prismacolor Lavender, Rouge, White, Chartreuse, Aquamarine and Flesh Tone

Markers/Pens: White Jelly Roll Pen by Uchida

Other: Magazine Font Stickers by Rusty Pickle

INSTRUCTIONS
1. Stamp image on cardstock in green ink.
2. Stamp No. 1 image on scrap cardstock in Peacock. Trim close and set aside.
3. Color left image with pencils; accent hair with pink and lavender, color edge in same colors.
4. Color flesh tones on face, accent with pink and lavender.
5. Scribble with white pencil in dark shadowed area behind boy as shown.
6. Glue No.1 image at slight angle over rectangle shape. Add "b.o.y." sticker.
7. Accent with white gel pen along border.

The Waltz
Carlene Federer

MATERIALS
Rubber Stamps: Dance by Inkadinkado

Dye Inkpads: Archival Sepia

Papers: Cardstock

Other: Embossing Powders; Image by ARTchix Studio

INSTRUCTIONS
1. Stamp dance image onto cardstock; emboss with clear powder.
2. Computer-generate words, print and cut out.
3. Add image; ink edge of words and adhere to card; ink edges of ATC.

1 Life 1 Day 1 Moment
Amy Wellenstein

MATERIALS
Rubber Stamps: Wings Plate by PaperArtsy; Shrine by Stampers Anonymous; Phrase by Creative Imaginations

Pigment Inkpads: VersaFine Onyx Black

Dye Inkpads: Adirondack Rust

Papers: White Cardstock; Gumballs and Aged & Confused Sublime Collection by BasicGrey

Other: Foam Tape

INSTRUCTIONS
1. Stamp woman in black ink on white cardstock.
2. Stamp Shrine on patterned cardstock, cut out window.
3. Stamp 1 LIFE 1 DAY 1 MOMENT in rust ink along the left side.
4. Layer panels using foam tape.

Wild Horses

Jean Hawkins

MATERIALS

Rubber Stamps: Three Beauties and Three Graces by Coronado Island; Aztec Border by Stampabilities

Dye Inkpads: Memories Black; Tea Dye and Fired Brick Distress Inks

Papers: Ivory Cardstock; Brown Kraft Paper

Colored Pencils: Prismacolor

Other: Brown Eyelets; Ribbons

Tools: Sponges; Japanese Screw Punch; Eyelet Setter

INSTRUCTIONS

1. Sponge Distress Inks onto ivory cardstock; stamp Aztec Border in black ink; color.
2. Stamp Three Graces horse image onto kraft paper, tear around edge.
3. Stamp Three Beauties onto kraft paper, cut out.
4. Glue to card and color background as shown; punch holes, set eyelets, tie on ribbons.

Victorian Purse

Kathy Plante

MATERIALS

Rubber Stamps: Purse by Me and Carrie Lou; Tiny Kiss and Frame by All Night Media/Plaid

Pigment Inkpads: ColorBox Lava Black and Red

Papers: Glossy White Cardstock; Black Cardstock

Markers/Pens: Gold Leafing Pen by Krylon

Other: Poly Shrink; Paper Cords; Clear Embossing Powder; JudiKins Diamond Glaze; Lavender Fabric Paper; Gold Thread; Terra Cotta, Cranberry, Lettuce, Denim Alcohol Inks and Blending Solution by Adirondack

Tools: Heat Tool; 1/16" Hole Punch; Key Punch; Circle Punch

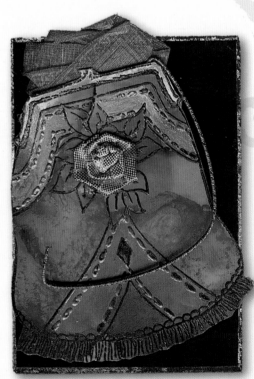

INSTRUCTIONS

1. Squeeze several drops of alcohol inks and several drops from gold pen onto glossy paper, tilt paper allowing inks to run together.
2. Stamp purse image; cutout, emboss and embellish as shown.
3. Punch keys and circles out of poly shrink, follow manufacturer's directions to shrink. Attach with gold thread.
4. Stamp, cut out and fold handkerchief into the purse. Attach; add keys. Adhere to ATC; outline with gold pen.

Dream

Kelly Lunceford

MATERIALS

Rubber Stamps: Express It by Making Memories; Life's Journey Stamp Set by K&Company

Dye Inkpads: StazOn Timber Brown; Black Inkstone and Crimson Red by Rubber Stampede

Pigment Inkpads: Coffee Bean by Rubber Stampede

Papers: Cardstock

Pastels/Chalks: Various Chalks

Other: Crimson Walnut Paper Wash by 7gypsies; Brads; Ribbons

Tools: ¹/₁₆" Hole Punch; Blender Pen

INSTRUCTIONS

1. Randomly stamp key image, cut kraft paper and tear to fit as shown, distress, attach brad.
2. Stamp dream image, color with chalk, blend with blender pen, attach.
3. Drop color wash randomly onto card, rub into card.
4. Stamp key image, color with chalk, attach ribbon.
5. Stamp postmark image and clock images, cut out postmark and attach.
6. Cut out clock, distress edges, attach to card, add brads.
7. Stamp "enjoy the journey", trim and attach. Distress entire card to finish.

Life: A Table of Contents

Janet Klein

MATERIALS

Rubber Stamps: Rectangles Block by Stampotique Originals

Dye Inkpads: Archival Jet Black

Papers: Cardstock; Book Text; Black Paper

Paints: White Acrylic Paint

Pastels/Chalks: Portfolio Series Water Soluble Oil Pastels

Colored Pencils: Prismacolor

Markers/Pens: PITT Artist Pen, White Gel Pen

Tools: Paintbrush; Hole Punch

INSTRUCTIONS

1. Computer-generate assorted words for journal contents, cut out.
2. Trim text and glue to ATC. Scribble pastels on edge of card, blend with damp brush.
3. Stamp block image, adhere to card, accent with colored pencils.
4. Scribble faux script on black paper with white gel pen, edge card with pencil, punch openings.

News Break

Jill Haglund

MATERIALS

Rubber Stamps: Bird by Stampers Anonymous

Dye Inkpads: India Ink Black by Stewart Superior

Pastels/Chalks: Portfolio Series Water Soluble Oil Pastels

Colored Pencils: Watercolor Pencils; Colored Pencils

Markers/Pens: Aqua PITT Artist Pen

Other: Gesso by Golden; Playing Card

Tools: Small Watercolor Brush

INSTRUCTIONS

1. Gesso playing card, let dry.
2. Color with colored pencils and watercolor pencils and touch areas lightly with a wet paintbrush to enhance color.
3. Paint card in blue acrylic. Rub oil pastels as shown. Scribble aqua PITT pen for border.
4. Cut out bird and adhere.

What You See
Ginny Carter Smallenberg

MATERIALS

Rubber Stamps: Checkerboard and Phrase by Stampers Anonymous

Pigment Inkpads: ColorBox Green and Black

Papers: Cardstock

Other: Clown Cutout; Gel Medium

INSTRUCTIONS

1. Mask ATC and rub green ink onto half of cut cardstock.
2. Stamp checkerboard image and "BEING" in black.
3. Adhere cutout clown with gel medium.
4. Stamp "what you see"; cover with gel medium.

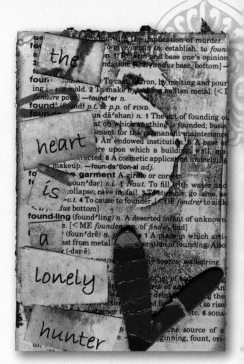

The Heart is a Lonely Hunter
Carlene Federer

MATERIALS

Rubber Stamps: Face by PaperArtsy

Dye Inkpads: StazOn Jet Black

Papers: Cardstock

Other: Chipboard Heart by Heidi Swapp; Vintage Dictionary Page; Burgundy Glitter Pen

INSTRUCTIONS

1. Adhere vintage dictionary paper to cardstock; stamp image over paper.
2. Computer-generate words; adhere to card.
3. Circle word "found" and add chipboard heart.

Carte Postale and Libro Primo
Wendy Sullivan

MATERIALS

Rubber Stamps: Script Letter and Penmanship Backgrounds by Penny Black; Dog by Stamp Francisco; Dancers by Cherry Pie; Flower by Hampton Art; Art, Carte Postale, Beetle and Words (source unknown)

Dye Inkpads: Archival Coffee; Brilliance Graphite Black; StazOn Jet Black

Papers: Cardstock; Parisian Stripes by Sharon Soneff of Sonnets Studios

Paints: Gold Moonglow Glitz Spritz by Lindy's Stamp Gang; Blue Spray Dye (homemade)*

Markers/Pens: Gold Marker by Krylon

Other: Gold Metal Tape; White Floral Eyelet; TransparencyTools: Eyelet Setter; Hole Punch; Stipple Brush

INSTRUCTIONS

1. Cut cardstocks to size. Lightly spritz blue cardstock with Moonglow and blue dye for a mottled effect.
2. Stamp backgrounds and words on blue and ivory cardstocks, layer.
3. Cut equal sized squares of Parisian striped paper and transparency.
4. Stamp image on transparency with StazOn. Sandwich paper and transparency together and trim in metal tape as shown.
5. Punch hole, add eyelet.

Homemade Spray Dye: Add 2 teaspoons of powdered fabric dye (like RIT) to a 2-ounce spray bottle and fill with warm distilled water. Shake and spray! Add more dye for a darker, richer spritz and mix colors to create custom sprays!

Dreamy Artist

Corrine Byers

MATERIALS

Rubber Stamps: Eiffel Tower by Impression Obsession; Diffusion by Hampton Art; Lady with Umbrella by Articus Studio

Dye Inkpads: StazOn Black

Paper: Cardstock

Pastels/Chalks: Various Chalks

Marker/Pens: Gold Medium Point Marker

INSTRUCTIONS

1. Apply chalks randomly on cardstock; stamp images.
2. Outline card with gold marker.

Bicyclette

Deb Lewis

MATERIALS

Rubber Stamps: Script by Rubber Baby Buggy Bumpers

Dye Inkpads: Archival Sepia

Papers: Cardstock; Decorative Tissue Paper; Vintage Text Pages

Other: Transparency; Vintage Photograph; Gesso

INSTRUCTIONS

1. Create layers on cardstock by gluing down sheer layers of tissue and text.
2. Attach transparency and vintage photograph; overstamp with script in sepia ink.
3. Paint with gesso, adhere computer-generated word; ink edges with sepia.

D is for Dream

Deb Lewis

MATERIALS

Dye Inkpads: Archival Sepia

Papers: White and Black Cardstock; Vintage French Dictionary Pages; Kraft Paper

Other: Vintage Photograph; Clipart Butterfly; "A" Bubble; Clover

INSTRUCTIONS

1. Ink edges of ATC vintage pages to age; layer pages onto cardstock.
2. Cut large letter "D" from black cardstock.
3. Adhere vintage photograph, letter and butterfly.

Fish Face

*(One of a series of 4 for
a Faces or Masks theme swap)*

Christy Hawkins

MATERIALS

Rubber Stamps: Big Pompano by Fred B. Mullett; Buttons Pixie Alphabet by PSX

Pigment Inkpads: VersaColor Black and Cement

Dye Inkpads: Seashells Starfish Green

Papers: Fine Grain Watercolor Paper; Black Cardstock

Paints: Prang Oval 8 Watercolors; Grumbacher Chinese White Watercolor

Other: Embossing Powders; Aleene's Paper Glaze by Duncan

Tools: Watercolor Brushes; Heat Tool; Sponge Daubers by Tsukineko

INSTRUCTIONS

1. Stamp images on watercolor paper; paint.
2. Color background with a wash of blue, let dry.
3. Add accents on fins with white watercolor straight from tube; cover eye with glaze.
4. Stamp "fish face" as shown; adhere to black cardstock.

Noble Face

Christy Hawkins

MATERIALS

Rubber Stamps: Lion by Art Impressions; Magnetic Alphabet Stamps by Making Memories

Dye Inkpads: Memories Brown and Midnight Blue

Papers: Black and White Cardstock

Colored Pencils: Prismacolor Goldenrod, Yellow Ochre and Terra Cotta

Other: Aleene's Paper Glaze by Duncan; Brads

Tools: Blender Pen

INSTRUCTIONS

1. Stamp face portion of lion image in brown ink on white paper; let dry, color, add glaze to eye.
2. Stamp "noble face" with the alphabet stamps.
3. Layer onto black cardstock and trim to ATC size.
4. Pierce the paper and add brads.

Little Corset

Judith Godwin

MATERIALS

Rubber Stamps: Ticking by B Line Designs; Decorative Corset by Hampton Art

Pigment Inkpads: Brilliance Mediterranean Blue

Dye Inkpads: StazOn Jet Black

Papers: Off-White, Vanilla and White Cardstock

Paints: Watercolors

Other: Fiber; Lace Scrap; Yellow Ruler Ribbon; Washer; Brads; Tags

Tools: 1/16" Hole Punch; Paintbrush

INSTRUCTIONS

1. Stamp ticking background in Mediterranean blue on off-white cardstock.
2. Paint vanilla cardstock in watercolors as shown, let dry.
3. Stamp corset in black ink on painted cardstock, cut out corset.
4. Wrap fibers around waist several times and tie a knot.
5. Wrap lace around ticking background at a diagonal angle, tape to back.
6. Wrap ribbon around washer, punch hole, insert brads in ribbon.
7. Adhere corset to cardstock with foam tape.
8. Cover back with white cardstock.

Zebra Face

Christy Hawkins

MATERIALS

Rubber Stamps: Zebra by Great Impressions; Alphabet Graven Tiny by Ma Vinci's Reliquary

Dye Inkpads: Memories Black; Adirondack Lettuce

Papers: Black and White Cardstock

Other: Aleene's Paper Glaze by Duncan; Colored, Shaped Brads

INSTRUCTIONS

1. Cut white paper slightly smaller than ATC size; stamp Zebra in black, let dry.
2. Cover eyes with glaze, stamp "zebra face" in green.
3. Layer onto black cardstock and trim to ATC size.
4. Pierce holes and add brads.

Fowl Face

Christy Hawkins

MATERIALS

Rubber Stamps: Rooster by Sandi Miller Art Stamps; Alphabet Graven Tiny by Ma Vinci's Reliquary

Dye Inkpads: Memories Black; Adirondack Red Pepper

Papers: Black and White Cardstock

Markers/Pens: Various Markers

Other: Wire Mesh; Mini Brads; Aleene's Paper Glaze by Duncan

INSTRUCTIONS

1. Cut white cardstock slightly smaller than ATC size.
2. Stamp head and chest portion of Rooster in black ink; let dry, color with markers.
3. Tear away the upper left corner as shown; stamp "fowl face" in red.
4. Cut a strip of wire mesh and combine with torn piece; tape in place.
5. Adhere entire image to black cardstock cut to ATC size.
6. Pierce the card and add mini brads to secure wire mesh.
7. Add a touch of glaze to the eye and fill the beak.

Women are Like Buttons

Judy Godwin

MATERIALS

Rubber Stamps: Phrase and Buttons (source unknown)

Dye Inkpads: StazOn Timber Brown and Jet Black

Paper: Light and Dark Brown Cardstock; Embossed Button by K&Company

Other: Vintage Buttons

Tools: Craft Knife; Mat

INSTRUCTIONS

1. Slit dark brown cardstock with craft knife; slip through button-stamped and trimmed paper.
2. Adhere inked, embossed button paper to top.
3. Tear small piece of light brown paper; ink edges and stamp phrase, glue to front.

GARDEN JOURNAL

gar·den (gär′dən), n. 1. piece of ground used for growing ables, herbs, flowers, or fruit le and delightful spot region. —v. take care journal (jér′nəl), n 2. account of what hap one thinks or notices

London
Ginny Carter Smallenburg

MATERIALS

Rubber Stamps: Script by Stampers Anonymous

Dye Inkpads: StazOn Jet Black

Papers: Ivory and Brown Cardstock; Green Scrap Paper

Other: Vintage Image

INSTRUCTIONS

1. Cover cardstock with green paper; stamp script.
2. Adhere strip of dark brown cardstock; glue image on top, smooth with bone folder.

TO STAMP
OR NOT TO STAMP.
THAT IS THE QUEST'

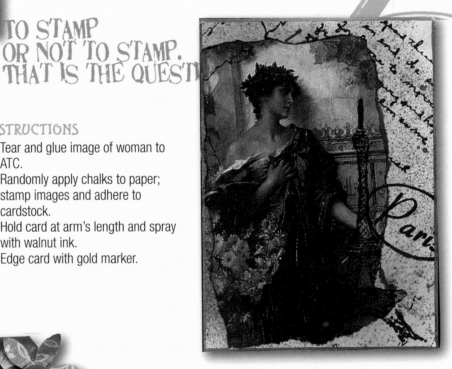

Provence & Paris

Corrine Byers

MATERIALS

Rubber Stamps: Diffusion by Hampton Art; Eiffel Tower by Impression Obsession; Paris (source unknown)

Dye Inkpads: StazOn Black

Papers: Cream Cardstock; Collage Woman Patterned Paper (source unknown)

Pastels/Chalks: Various Chalks

Markers/Pens: Gold Marker

Other: Walnut Ink Spray

INSTRUCTIONS

1. Tear and glue image of woman to ATC.
2. Randomly apply chalks to paper; stamp images and adhere to cardstock.
3. Hold card at arm's length and spray with walnut ink.
4. Edge card with gold marker.

FIRST CLASS

What is Your Story
Sharon Wisely

MATERIALS

Rubber Stamps: Unmounted Stamps by Red Lead PaperWorks

Dye Inkpads: StazOn Jet Black

Papers: Romani by BasicGrey; Vellum

Other: Red Pom Pom; White Tag

Tools: Flower Punch; Sewing Machine; Scallop Scissors

INSTRUCTIONS

1. Stamp image on cardstock in black ink.
2. Cut vellum; trim one edge with scallop scissors, stitch to ATC on three sides to form pocket.
3. Cut cardstock, stamp image, glue to tag.
4. Punch flower from cardstock; glue pom pom to flower, glue flower to tag.
5. Stamp "what is your story" on cardstock, cut out and glue to vellum pocket.

Yesterday

Deb Lewis

MATERIALS

Dye Inkpads: Archival Sepia

Papers: Cardstock; Vintage French Dictionary Text; Embossed Wallpaper

Other: Rusting Medium; Vintage Buttons; Vintage Photograph

INSTRUCTIONS

1. Treat wallpaper with rusting medium and glue to cardstock.
2. Attach vintage photograph and buttons; ink edges of card with sepia ink.

Mr. Bear

Deb Lewis

MATERIALS

Dye Inkpads: Archival Sepia

Papers: Cardstock; Vintage Text Paper; Embossed Button Paper by K&Company

Other: Vintage Photograph; Butterfly Wings; Heart-Shaped Metal Brad; Vintage Buttons; Ribbon; Flower

INSTRUCTIONS

1. Ink edges of text paper to age; glue to button paper and trim.
2. Layer onto cardstock.
3. Glue vintage girl. Adhere flower and button on hat.
4. Add ribbon snippets and buttons to side.

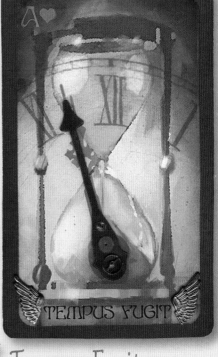

Tempus Fugit

Deb Lewis

MATERIALS

Papers: Cardstock

Other: Watercolor Painting of Hourglass; Clock Image; Brass Wings; Vintage Copper Clock Hour Hand; Vintage Watch Parts

INSTRUCTIONS

1. Scan watercolor painting.
2. Use Photoshop or similar program to overlay image of clock onto scanned painting.
3. Print out image; glue to cardstock, attach all metal embellishments.

Dance and Sing

Christy Hawkins

MATERIALS

Rubber Stamps: Ethnic Figures by Another Stamp Company; Music by Great Impressions

Dye Inkpads: Memories Black

Papers: Cardstock and Vellum by Provo Craft

Colored Pencils: Prismacolor

Other: Post-it Notes; Computer Font "Journaling" by Creating Keepsakes

INSTRUCTIONS

1. Cut and layer colored cardstock.
2. Stamp the three figures as shown.
3. Stamp bottom figure on Post-it, cut out to make mask. Mask the bottomfigure and stamp music image across the bottom of the card.
4. Color figures with Prismacolor pencils.
5. Print the Zimbabwe proverb on vellum. Allow to dry, cut out and adhere.

Fashion in Watercolors

Wendy Sullivan

MATERIALS

Rubber Stamps: Women by Hampton Art; French Text by Non Sequitur; Klimt Swirls by Cherry Pie; Script by All Night Media/Plaid

Dye Inkpads: Brilliance Graphite Black

Papers: Cardstock; Watercolor Paper

Markers/Pens: Various Markers

Tools: Watercolor Brush; Foam Paper Plate; Heat Tool

INSTRUCTIONS

1. Stamp images as shown on pre-cut watercolor paper.
2. Scribble the markers onto dry foam paper plate; pick up colors with a brush and apply to image, blend as desired.

One Penny

Jill Haglund

MATERIALS

Rubber Stamps: Phrase by PaperArtsy

Pigment Inkpads: ColorBox Olive Green; Memories Black, Barn Red and Green

Papers: Glossy Cardstock

Other: Penny; Pencil; Coffee Insulator With Holes; Green, Yellow and Orange Alcohol Inks

Tools: Blender Pen

INSTRUCTIONS

1. Drop alcohol inks on back of glossy paper; blend with pen. Move color around until paper is coated in a large enough area to cut out an ATC.
2. Place the coffee insulator with holes on top of ATC; dab through holes with inkpad, then use eraser tip to stamp dots.
3. Stamp phrase, adhere penny.

Them Kids with the Hats

Janet Klein

MATERIALS

Rubber Stamps: Toni's Kids by Stampotique Originals

Pigment Inkpads: Dauber Duos Pinks, Blue and Lavender

Dye Inkpads: Archival Jet Black

Papers: Cardstock; Book Page; Newsprint; Scraps of Script and Patterned Papers

Paints: Diluted White Acrylic; Green Acrylic; Watercolors

Pastels/Chalks: Portfolio Series Water Soluble Oil Pastels

Colored Pencils: Prismacolor Violet, Orange, Lime and White

Tools: Small Flat Paintbrush; Corner Punch; Heat Tool

INSTRUCTIONS

1. Trim portion of text and glue to cardstock; scribble aqua pastel around edge of card.
2. Add white pastel toward the inside of card; blend with a wet brush, let dry.
3. Stamp Toni's Kids in black on scrap. Let dry, cut out and paint with watercolors. Let dry, accent with colored pencils.
4. Stamp Dauber Duos randomly over ATC, heat set.
5. Tear scrap of script, glue at bottom of card. Adhere kids image and hats.
6. Draw border with aqua pencil. Use fingertip to apply green paint accent on card edge.

Love Story

Carlene Federer

MATERIALS

Rubber Stamps: Man by PaperArtsy; Border by Stampers Anonymous

Pigment Inkpads: StazOn Jet Black; ColorBox Orange

Papers: Cardstock

Other: Ribbons; Vintage Female Image by ARTchix Studio

Tools: Xacto Knife; Stapler

INSTRUCTIONS

1. Stamp man image in black and border image in orange onto cardstock.
2. Using Xacto knife, cut around images as shown; staple on ribbons.

My Smile

Christy Hawkins

MATERIALS

Rubber Stamps: Source of Joy by Paperbag Studios; Giggles by Rubbermoon; Numbers by Making Memories

Dye Inkpads: StazOn Jet Black

Papers: Red Cardstock; Star Patterned Paper by Paper Adventures

Other: Tag; Brad; Photo

INSTRUCTIONS

1. Tear and layer patterned paper as shown, add photo.
2. Stamp quote, tear and adhere. Computer-generate text, print out, cut into strips and adhere.
3. Stamp "giggle" on tag and adhere with brad.

Queen of the Night

Carlene Federer

MATERIALS

Rubber Stamps: Postmodern Design
Dye Inkpads: StazOn Jet Black
Papers: Cardstock
Other: Image and Wings by ARTchix Studios; Rhinestones
Tools: Dymo Label Maker

INSTRUCTIONS

1. Stamp image on cardstock, adhere woman image, add wings.
2. Type title with label maker.
3. Adhere rhinestones and label to card.

Fly Away with Me

Sharon Wisely

MATERIALS

Rubber Stamps: Unmounted Stamps by Red Lead PaperWorks
Dye Inkpads: StazOn Jet Black
Papers: Romani by BasicGrey
Other: Foam Tape
Tools: Circle Punch

INSTRUCTIONS

1. Stamp wing and face image on cardstock in black ink.
2. On separate cardstock, stamp wing and cut out, stamp face and punch out.
3. Overlay the cut out wing and glue the left edge of wing on top of the stamped wing for dimension.
4. Overlay and adhere the stamped circle on top of stamped face with foam tape.

Begin Joy

Roben-Marie Smith

MATERIALS

Rubber Stamps: Joy Block by Paperbag Studios
Dye Inkpads: Adirondack Mushroom
Papers: Cartaceo Classic Pink by Daisy D's; DK Sepia Scroll by American Traditional Designs
Other: Life's Journey Bubble Word by K&Company; Blossoms by Making Memories; Snaps; Playing Card
Tools: 1/16" Hole Punch

INSTRUCTIONS

1. Cover playing card with patterned paper and trim to size.
2. Stamp Joy Block on pink paper, trim and adhere.
3. Adhere bubble word to flower with glue dot, adhere to card.
4. Add snaps to finish.

trust your crazy ideas...

No 22545

Amy Wellenstein

MATERIALS

Rubber Stamps: Women and Numbers by Stampotique Originals; Chicken Wire by Great Impressions

Pigment Inkpads: VersaMark WaterMark; VersaFine Onyx Black

Pastels/Chalks: Various Chalks

Other: Post-it Notes

INSTRUCTIONS

1. Stamp women images, stamp again and cut out for mask.
2. Mask women images and overstamp chicken wire background in VersaMark WaterMark. Wait two minutes
3. With masks still in place, rub chalk over card.
4. Remove mask, stamp numbers, color women with chalks.

Young Old – Just Words

Sharon Wisely

MATERIALS

Rubber Stamps: Unmounted Stamps by Red Lead PaperWorks

Dye Inkpads: StazOn Jet Black

Papers: Romani by BasicGrey

Other: Metal-Rimmed Circle Tag; Red Eyelet; Red Pom Pom

Tools: Eyelet Setter; 1/8" Punch

INSTRUCTIONS

1. Stamp image on cardstock in black ink.
2. Stamp cut starburst shape from another piece of patterned cardstock, glue to top of card.
3. Set eyelet in circle tag; stamp image, glue pom pom to party hat.

No. 7821

Roben-Marie Smith

MATERIALS

Rubber Stamps: Sentiments by Paperbag Studios

Dye Inkpads: VersaFine Onyx Black

Papers: Classic Pink Plaid by Daisy D's; Pink Stripe by Rusty Pickle

Other: Rick Rack; Vintage Buttons; Playing Card

INSTRUCTIONS

1. Cover card with plaid paper. Stamp image on striped paper, adhere to card.
2. Glue rick rack to card; add buttons with glue dots.

We Don't Stop Playing

Ginny Carter Smallenburg

MATERIALS

Rubber Stamps: Stampers Anonymous
Dye Inkpads: Marvy Matchables
Ochre, Pale Green, Wine and Black
Paper: White and Ivory Cardstock
Other: Clip Art

INSTRUCTIONS

1. Stamp all backgrounds as shown, stamp phrases.
2. Cut out clip art and adhere over background; smooth with bone folder.

Love in the Evening

Jane Maley

MATERIALS

Rubber Stamps: Caroline from Cologne by The Queen's Dresser Drawers

Dye Inkpads: StazOn Olive Green

Papers: White Glossy Cardstock

Other: Clock Charm; Rhinestone Stickers; Alphabet Stickers by Making Memories; Craft Sheet; Alcohol Inks in Wild Plum, Terracotta and Butterscotch; JudiKins Diamond Glaze

INSTRUCTIONS

1. Drop alcohol inks onto craft sheet, place cardstock on craft sheet and move in a circular motion until inked, cut out ATC.
2. Stamp image and add elements as shown.

Believe in your dreams.

Gypsy Dream

Jane Maley

MATERIALS

Rubber Stamps: Roxana by Invoke Arts; Late Night Thoughts by Stampers Anonymous; Diamond by Hero Arts

Papers: Cardstock

Dye Inkpads: StazOn Vibrant Violet, Cactus Green, Teal Blue, Cherry Pink, Sunflower Yellow and Jet Black

Other: Colored Gem Brads; Star Brads

Tools: Cosmetic Sponge; Long-Reach ¹/₁₆" Punch

INSTRUCTIONS

1. Randomly apply inks to card with sponge.
2. Stamp Roxana in black ink and Late Night Thoughts in teal.
3. Stamp edges of card with tips only of diamond image.
4. Punch holes along the crown and on each ear.
5. Insert star brads along the crown and gemstone brads on ears.

Artist Trading Card

Planet Paris

Corrine Byers

MATERIALS

Rubber Stamps: Articus Studio; Paris Image (source unknown)

Dye Inkpads: Summer Sun by Stampin' Up; Seashells Conch Shell, Fired Brick Distress Ink

Markers/Pens: Gold Marker by Pilot

Other: Tim Holtz Distressables Cutable Strips; Stampboard

Tools: ColorBox Stylus

INSTRUCTIONS

1. Apply inks on stampboard with stylus as shown, using lighter colors first.
2. Stamp image, add word strip. Edge with gold marker, add photo turn to finish.

It's the simple joys, the simple pleasures the heart remembers and dearly treasures.

Happy Holidays
Roben-Marie Smith

MATERIALS

Rubber Stamps: Music Tree by Paperbag Studios

Dye Inkpads: VersaFine Onyx Black

Papers: Patterned Paper by Designs by Reminisce

Other: Printed Twill by 7gypsies; Hymnal Page; Playing Cards

Tools: Corner Edger

INSTRUCTIONS

1. Glue hymnal paper to ATC sized cardstock.
2. Stamp Music Tree to patterned paper as shown, trim edges of Music Tree card with edging tool.
3. Using double-sided tape, attach Music Tree card to hymnal card. Staple on twill to finish.

Rosie
Lisa Gifford

MATERIALS

Rubber Stamps: Ladies Night and Woman by The Stampsmith

Dye Inkpads: StazOn Jet Black, Magenta and Gold

Papers: Cardstock; Glossy Cardstock, Book Text; Mulberry Paper

Markers/Pens: Markers

Other: Ribbon; Wax; Glitter; Button; Brad

Tools: 1/16" Punch

INSTRUCTIONS

1. Stamp Ladies Night on card, stamp woman image on glossy cardstock, color and cut out.
2. Punch two holes in ATC; thread and tie ribbon.
3. Adhere mulberry paper and layer woman image.
4. Cover button with glue, add glitter; adhere.

Believe
Lisa Gifford

MATERIALS

Rubber Stamps: Fairy Image by The Stampsmith; Word Image (source unknown)

Dye Inkpads: StazOn Jet Black; Marvy Rosemarie

Papers: Pink Cardstock; Scrapbook Papers

Other: Red Brad; Circle Clip; Playing Card

Tools: Textured Brayer

INSTRUCTIONS

1. Stamp fairy image, mat onto cardstock.
2. Brayer background on prepared playing card; add torn scrap paper, with brad.
3. Adhere fairy image, add clip
4. Stamp word to finish.

WE ARE THE
MUSIC MAKERS,
AND WE ARE
THE DREAMERS
OF DREAMS.

American Goths

Karen Shafer

MATERIALS

Rubber Stamps: American Gothic by Museum Stamps; Crackle Background by JudiKins

Dye Inkpads: StazOn Jet Black; Archival Sepia and Maroon

Papers: Red and White Cardstock; Black Paper; Assorted Papers

Colored Pencils: Various Colors

Other: Doll Hair

INSTRUCTIONS

1. Color white cardstock with sepia and maroon inks.
2. Stamp crackle background on red cardstock.
3. Stamp American Gothic on various papers for face and clothing. Color background barn with pencils.
4. Assemble clothing and glue to head. Trim and mat to black paper; adhere words and image with foam tape

Bus Stop

Jill Haglund

MATERIALS

Rubber Stamps: Children and Script by Paperbag Studios

Pigment Inkpads: VersaFine Onyx Black

Dye Inkpads: StazOn Timber Brown

Papers: Studio K by K&Company; Cardstock

Colored Pencils: Prismacolor

Other: Post-it Notes; Playing Card

INSTRUCTIONS

1. Stamp children image on cardstock. Stamp again to make a mask. Mask over legs and stamp script as shown.
2. Remove mask, color children with pencils.
3. Adhere to patterned paper, glue to playing card, trim.

He Dreamed of Mermaids

Carlene Federer

MATERIALS

Rubber Stamps: PaperArtsy

Dye Inkpads: Archival Sepia

Papers: Cardstock

Paints: Teal Zircon Twinkling H2O's

Other: Mermaid Image by ARTchix Studio; Little Boy Image; Music Paper; Rhinestone; Aleene's Paper Glaze by Duncan

INSTRUCTIONS

1. Paint ATC with Teal Zircon, let dry.
2. Add music paper, mermaid and boy image.
3. Computer-generate words, adhere to ATC.
4. Add thick layer of paper glaze, let dry.
5. Adhere rhinestone.

Don't Be Shy Wear Fancy Clothes

Jill Haglund

MATERIALS

Rubber Stamps: Hip Chick, Don't Be Shy and Wear Fancy Clothes by Rubbermoon; Spatter by Stampotique Originals

Pigment Inkpads: VersaFine Onyx Black

Dye Inkpads: Marvy Matchables Light Blue

Papers: Pink, Ivory and White Cardstock; Paradise Punch Dotted Line by Doodlebug Designs; Beach II by Memories Complete

Colored Pencils: Various Colors

Other: Post-it Notes; Blue Staples

INSTRUCTIONS:

1. Stamp Hip Chick on ivory cardstock.
2. Stamp again onto patterned papers; cut out skirt from one and jacket/hat from the other.
3. Glue papers to ATC.
4. Stamp Hip Chick again on a Post-it Note for mask.
5. Cut out image and use as a mask; stamp Spatter in Light Blue, lift mask.
6. Stamp Don't be Shy and Wear Fancy Clothes onto white cardstock, cut out, mat onto pink cardstock. Adhere.

Just swimmin' by to say, 'Hi!'

Just Swimming By

Deanna Furey

MATERIALS

Rubber Stamps: Retro Fish by JudiKins; Phrase by My Sentiments Exactly

Pigment Inkpads: Brilliance Graphite Black; Pearlescent Coral

Papers: Pink Paper; Glitter Paper and Striped Paper Recycled from Greeting Card

Other: Sequences

INSTRUCTIONS

1. Stamp phrase onto striped paper in black ink; stamp fish onto pink paper in pink ink.
2. Cut out and glue to striped paper; adhere sequences.
3. Mat with glitter paper and glue to pink paper.

Oh So Pretty
from a Series of 4 Dainty Things

Christy Hawkins

MATERIALS

Rubber Stamps: Compact by Me & Carrie Lou; Oh So Pretty by Rubbermoon

Dye Inkpads: Memories Black

Papers: Pink and White Cardstock; Patterned Paper by Sonburn

Paints: Chiffon Pink, Green Tea, and Heavenly White Twinkling H2O's

Markers/Pens: Rose Zig Writer by EK Success

Other: JudiKins Diamond Glaze; Foam Tape

Tools: Small Watercolor Brush

INSTRUCTIONS

1. Edge pink cardstock with a torn strip of print paper, stamp phrase in black ink.
2. Stamp Compact on white cardstock, color with Twinkling H2O's and Zig Writer.
3. Apply Diamond Glaze to clasp, hinge and flowers.
4. Let paint and glaze dry thoroughly; cut out Compact, mount on ATC with foam tape.

oh, so pretty

Smells Sweet from a Series of 4 Dainty Things
Christy Hawkins

MATERIALS
Rubber Stamps: Perfume Bottle by Me & Carrie Lou; Sweetness by Rubbermoon

Dye Inkpads: Memories Black

Papers: Pink and White Cardstock; Patterned Paper by Sonburn

Paints: Chiffon Pink, Green Tea, Yellow Rose and Buttercup Twinkling H2O's

Markers/Pens: Candy Pink Zig Writer by EK Success

Other: JudiKins Diamond Glaze; Foam Tape

Tools: Small Watercolor Brush

INSTRUCTIONS
1. Edge pink cardstock with a torn strip of print paper; stamp word in black ink.
2. Stamp Perfume Bottle on white cardstock and color with Twinkling H2O's and Zig Writer.
3. Use Diamond Glaze on the top, the flower and the base of Perfume Bottle.
4. Let paint and glaze dry thoroughly; cut out Perfume Bottle, curl slightly, mount on ATC with foam tape.

sweetness

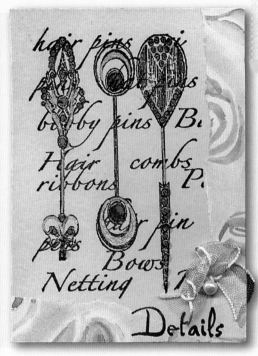

Details

Pretty Details from a Series of 4 Dainty Things
Christy Hawkins

MATERIALS
Rubber Stamps: Stickpins and Details (source unknown)

Dye Inkpads: Memories Black

Papers: Pink and White Cardstock; Patterned Paper by Sonburn

Markers/Pens: Silver Metallic and Silver Glitter Gel Pens by Sakura of America; Candy Pink Zig Writer by EK Success

Other: JudiKins Diamond Glaze; Fibers; Organdy Bow; Pearl Embellishment

INSTRUCTIONS
1. Stamp Stickpins in black ink; edge pink cardstock with a torn strip of print paper, stamp "Details" in black.
2. Color in some stones on stickpins; dot pink stones with Diamond Glaze, let dry.
3. Adhere bow, fibers and pearl embellishment.

Elegance from a Series of 4 Dainty Things
Christy Hawkins

MATERIALS
Rubber Stamps: Gloves by Impression Obsession; Elegance by Renaissance Art Stamps

Dye Inkpads: Memories Black

Papers: Pink and White Cardstock; Patterned Paper by Sonburn

Other: Fibers; Embroidery Floss; Foam Tape

Tools: Embroidery Needle

INSTRUCTIONS
1. Edge pink cardstock with a torn strip of print paper; stamp word in black ink.
2. Stamp Gloves on white cardstock in black ink; cut out.
3. Pierce dots on stamped design and stitch French knots as shown.
4. Mount gloves to ATC with foam tape.

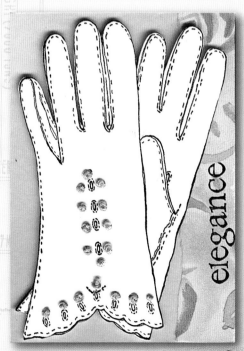

elegance

My Heart Belongs to Paris
Sue Roddis

MATERIALS

Rubber Stamps: Eiffel Tower by Tim Holtz for Stampers Anonymous; Pink Poodle Woman by Stamps Happen, Inc; ATC Letters by Catslife Press

Dye Inkpads: Scattered Straw, Worn Lipstick and Dusty Concord Distress Inks; Memories Black

Papers: White Semi-Gloss Cardstock; Black Cardstock

Markers/Pens: Pink Marvy Le Plume Marker; White Gel Pen

Other: I Kan Dee Twist Tie by Pebbles Inc.

Tools: Sponges; Heat Tool; Small Heart Punch

INSTRUCTIONS

1. Sponge white cardstock with Distress Inks, using lighter colors first, blend as you go. Dry with heat tool.
2. Stamp part of Eiffel Tower and woman images in black.
3. Color woman image with pink marker; highlight with white gel pen.
4. Sponge twist tie with inks and heat set; pierce two holes in the card, push twist tie through holes.
5. Stamp Eiffel Tower image on pink cardstock. Punch heart around the word "Paris"; add over twist tie.
6. Mount completed card onto black cardstock.

King of Hearts
Joyce Greenfield

MATERIALS

Rubber Stamps: Princess by The Stampsmith; Antique Typewriter Lower ABC by EK Success

Dye Inkpads: Adirondack Butterscotch, Rust, Caramel and Ginger; StazOn Jet Black

Papers: White Glossy Cardstock

Other: Gold Crown by Amy's Magic

Tools: Rubber Brayer; ATC Wizard Tool and Mechanical Pencil (comes with Wizard Tool) by European Papers; Metal Ruler; Wheel Cutter; Mat; Eraser; Stencil Brush; Corner Rounder

INSTRUCTIONS

1. Apply even pressure to stamp by rolling brayer in black ink, then on rubber for a smooth, even image.
2. Stamp "Princess" cat on glossy cardstock, center image and lightly mark edges of card using ATC Wizard Tool and pencil.
3. Cut out card using metal ruler, wheel cutter, and mat; erase any remaining pencil marks.
4. Age image by randomly applying dye inks with stencil brush (from lightest to darkest colors).
5. Round corners, stamp "K" and heart, adhere crown to cat.

Journey
Ginny Carter Smallenburg

MATERIALS

Dye Inkpads: StazOn Jet Black; Archival Sepia

Rubber Stamps: Script by Stampers Anonymous

Papers: Textured White Cardstock; Specialty Paper

Other: Vintage Image; Journey Plate by Stampers Anonymous

INSTRUCTIONS

1. Stamp text on textured white paper in black, let dry.
2. Stipple with brown ink to age.
3. Pierce two holes, add journey plate with mini brads.
4. Trim and layer onto red cardstock.
5. Layer vintage girl to specialty paper and adhere to front.

Family
Sharon Wisely

MATERIALS

Rubber Stamps: Unmounted Stamps by Red Lead PaperWorks

Dye Inkpads: StazOn Jet Black

Papers: Romani by BasicGrey; Vellum

Other: Pink Pom Pom

Tools: Flower Punch

INSTRUCTIONS

1. Stamp image on patterned cardstock in black ink.
2. Cut flower from another piece of cardstock; glue pom pom to flower, glue flower to ATC.

If you had Wings
Jill Hglund

MATERIALS

Rubber Stamps: Be Yourself by Tim Holtz for Stampers Anonymous

Dye Inkpads: India Ink Black by Stewart Superior

Papers: Ivory Bond Paper; White Cardstock; Newsprint

Paints: Twinkling H2O's; Titan Buff Acrylic by Golden

Other: Playing Card; Portfolio Series Water Soluble Oil Pastels; Fabric Swatch; Gesso; Eyelet; Button; Star; Brad

Tools: Eyelet Setter; 1/8" Hole Punch

INSTRUCTIONS

1. Cut newsprint and ivory bond paper slightly larger then ATC.
2. Adhere newsprint to prepared playing card, and trim.
3. Cover newsprint with thinned Titan Buff acrylic paint.
4. Stamp image on white cardstock, cut out, color with Twinkling H2O's, let dry.
5. Add highlights and border design with oil pastels.
6. Punch hole, set eyelet, pull through fabric swatch, adhere button.

Coffee at the Cafe
Nikki Cleary

MATERIALS

Rubber Stamps: Cup of Java (source unknown)

Dye Inkpads: India Ink Black by Stewart Superior

Papers: White Cardstock

Markers/Pens: Various Markers

Other: Rick Rack; Pink Thread; Button; Coffee; Mug

INSTRUCTIONS

1. Set bottom of coffee cup in hot coffee and then on card for circle stains as shown, let dry.
2. Stamp image in black; color with markers.
3. Sew thread through buttonholes, glue rick rack and button to front.

Treasured Seashore

Christy Hawkins

MATERIALS

Rubber Stamps: Sea Oats from Seaside by Stampin' Up!; Treasured by Rubbermoon

Dye Inkpads: Adirondack Stream and Caramel; StazOn Jet Black

Papers: Deep Water Pool by Provo Craft

Other: Playing Card; Whale Tale Charm by Fancifuls Inc.; Brad; Embroidery Floss; Kraft Colored Tissue Paper

Tools: Corner Rounder; Xyron

INSTRUCTIONS

1. Cut patterned paper into strips just slightly longer than ATC; run strips through Xyron machine.
2. Sand playing card to remove gloss.
3. Peel Xyron backing off paper and layer onto playing card, smooth, trim and round corners.
4. Tear tissue paper into strips and adhere to create "dunes".
5. Stamp Sea Oats in Caramel ink several times along the top of dune as shown.
6. Stamp Treasured in black.
7. Pierce card and hang whale tale charm using floss and brad.

Beach Post

Christy Hawkins

MATERIALS

Rubber Stamps: Shell Cube by Northwoods; Number Stamp by Ma Vinci's Reliquary

Pigment Inkpads: Brilliance Graphite Black

Dye Inkpads: Adirondack Stream, Bottle and Butterscotch

Papers: Cardstock; Patterned Paper by Creative Imaginations

Other: Faux Postage Template from Stampington & Company; Removable Painter's Tape

Tools: Xacto Knife; Ruler; Paper Trimmer; Stipple Brush; Perforator

INSTRUCTIONS

1. Cut black cardstock to ATC size, cut patterned paper slightly smaller, layer
2. Cut pieces of white or cream cardstock. Add faux postage template with removable tape.
3. Stipple background in Adirondack Stream ink.
4. Stamp the scallop shell image in Butterscotch and the starfish image in Bottle.
5. Remove the template and wipe it off. Add numbers in black ink. Let dry.
6. Use a perforator or other tool (such as a seamstress tracing wheel) to create the appearance of divisions between the "stamps". Lightly run the perforator across the inkpad several times to thoroughly ink; make the lines using a ruler.
7. Trim the faux postage, mount on prepared background.

Imagine a Vision

Christy Hawkins

MATERIALS

Rubber Stamps: Siren's Journal by Acey Deucy; Vision by Eclectic Omnibus

Dye Inkpads: StazOn Jet Black

Papers: Deep Water Pool by Provo Craft

Markers/Pens: Zig Scroll and Brush Markers in Evergreen, Sagebrush, Island Coral, Wheat, Peach Bliss, Pure Red, Splash, Coffee, Aubergine and Fuchsia

Other: Playing Card; Charm by Fancifuls Inc.; Brad;

Tools: Corner Rounder

INSTRUCTIONS

1. Cut patterned paper; run through Xyron machine.
2. Lightly sand one side of the playing card, adhere paper, smooth, trim to fit, round corners.
3. Stamp Siren's Journal in black, color image with brush markers; stamp Vision in black.
4. Pierce ATC; insert brad, hang charm from brad.

Wander

Christy Hawkins

MATERIALS

Rubber Stamps: Maiden Voyage by Acey Deucy; Map by Just for Fun; Wander Text by Hero Arts

Dye Inkpads: StazOn Jet Black; Adirondack Stream

Papers: Deep Water Pool and Vellum by Provo Craft

Other: Playing Card; Clear Microbeads by Darice

Tools: Corner Rounder; Xyron

INSTRUCTIONS

1. Cut patterned paper into strips slightly longer than ATC; run strips through Xyron machine.
2. Lightly sand one side of the playing card; adhere paper, smooth, trim to fit, round corners.
3. Stamp selected portion of map image in Stream ink, stamp Maiden Voyage in black.
4. Stamp phrase in black on vellum and trim into strips, run through Xyron.
5. Cut phrase to fit ATC as shown, smooth with bone folder.
6. Apply liquid glue along edges of text, shake on microbeads, remove excess beads; let dry.

Wander where there is no path

Think thoughts that make you happy

vision

treasured

5 5 5
5 5 5

Autumn Leaves

Joyce Kurtz

MATERIALS

Rubber Stamps: Leaf Art Impression and Whisper of Love by Hero Arts

Pigment Inkpads: ColorBox Canary; Scarlet, Olive, Red and Burnt Sienna

Dye Inkpads: StazOn Jet Black

Papers: Cream and Red Cardstock

Other: Wire; Beads; Timepiece Charm; Tag; Mini Silk Leave

Tools: Leaf Punch

INSTRUCTIONS

1. Stamp leaf randomly in various colored inks onto cream cardstock; stamp phrase in black.
2. Wrap wire, adding beads as you go; tape to back.
3. Add timepiece charm, mini silk leaf, small punched leaf and tag stamped with number.
4. Attach entire panel to red cardstock.

Directional Sunset

Corrine Byers

MATERIALS

Rubber Stamps: ArtRubber Stamps by Articus Studio

Dye Inkpads: StazOn Jet Black; Mustard Seed and Fired Brick Distress Inks

Markers/Pens: Gold Medium Point Marker by Pilot

Other: Tim Holtz Distressables Cutable Strips by Design Originals; Slide Mounts; Circular Paper Clip, Adhesive-Backed Square Rhinestones; Kamar Varnish by Krylon; Embossing Powder; Stampboard

Tools: ColorBox Stylus

INSTRUCTIONS

1. Apply inks to Stampboard with stylus, applying lighter, then darker shades.
2. Stamp image in black.
3. Adhere small square rhinestones to center of image and to center of circular clip.
4. Accent with gold marker; seal with varnish.

Time Journey

Corrine Byers

MATERIALS

Rubber Stamps: ArtRubber Stamps by Articus Studio

Dye Inkpads: StazOn Jet Black

Markers/Pens: Gold Medium Point Marker by Pilot

Other: Tim Holtz Distressable Cutable Strips by Design Originals; Kamar Varnish by Krylon; Stampboard

Tools: ColorBox Stylus

INSTRUCTIONS

1. Apply inks to stampboard with stylus, applying lighter, then darker shades.
2. Stamp image in black, color with markers, adhere strip words.
3. Edge with gold marker, seal with varnish.

What you once were and who you are now becoming is where the dance of life really takes place.

For Your Eyes Only

Amy Wellenstein

MATERIALS

Rubber Stamps: Face by Zettiology; For Your Eyes Only by Limited Edition

Pigment Inkpads: VersaFine Onyx Black

Papers: White Cardstock

Pastels/Chalks: Various Chalks

Colored Pencils: Prismacolor Blue and Lavender

INSTRUCTIONS

1. Stamp face image on white cardstock in black ink.
2. Color face with chalks, color eye with pencils.
3. Stamp For Your Eyes Only along the bottom in black.

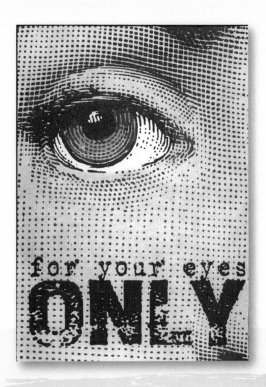

Send in the Clowns

Ginny Carter Smallenburg

MATERIALS

Rubber Stamps: Man, Clown and Background by Stampers Anonymous

Pigment Inkpads: India Ink Black by Stewart Superior

Paints: Watercolors

Colored Pencils: Prismacolor

Other: Post-it Notes; Number Sticker

Tools: Watercolor Brush

INSTRUCTIONS

1. Stamp small man and clown, stamp again on Post-it Note for mask.
2. Mask stamped images and stamp background.
3. Color images, add number sticker.

3 Wishes

Sharon Wisely

MATERIALS

Rubber Stamps: Unmounted Stamps by Red Lead PaperWorks

Dye Inkpads: StazOn Jet Black

Papers: Romani by BasicGrey; Vellum

Other: Metal-Rimmed Circle Tag; Red Eyelet; Pink Ribbon

Tools: 1/16" Circle Punch

INSTRUCTIONS

1. Stamp image on cardstock in black ink.
2. Cut starburst shape from separate piece of cardstock; punch a circle off-center in starburst. Glue starburst to ATC.
3. Cut strips of pape. Stamp words and adhere to card.
4. Stamp image onto circle tag; set eyelet, thread ribbon through eyelet, glue tag to front of ATC.

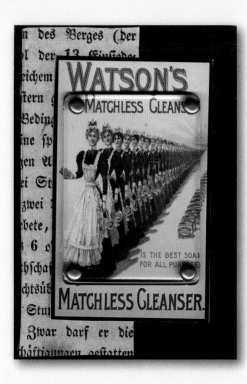

Watson's Matchless Cleanser

Ginny Carter Smallenburg

MATERIALS

Rubber Stamps: Text by Stampers Anonymous

Dye Inkpads: StazOn Jet Black

Papers: Ivory and Black Cardstock

Other: Acrylic Plate by Coffee Break Designs; Vintage Images by Stampers Anonymous

INSTRUCTIONS

1. Stamp background on ivory cardstock, layer onto half of black cardstock.
2. Adhere acrylic plate over image as shown.

Happy Birthday

Sharon Wisely

MATERIALS

Rubber Stamps: Unmounted Stamps by Red Lead PaperWorks

Dye Inkpads: StazOn Jet Black

Papers: Romani by BasicGrey; Vellum

Other: Red Round Photo Mount; Red Eyelet; Red Pom Pom; Pink Ribbon

Tools: Hole Punch; Sewing Machine; Scallop Scissors; Pinking Shears; Eyelet Setter

INSTRUCTIONS

1. Stamp image on cardstock in black ink.
2. Cut a piece of cardstock for tag; stamp image, punch hole, set eyelet.
3. Pull ribbon through eyelet and glue pom pom to tag.
4. Cut vellum square; trim one edge with scallop scissors, stitch vellum to ATC on three sides to form pocket.
5. Stamp image on cardstock and glue to inside of rounded photo mount, glue photo mount to vellum.
6. Trim edges with pinking shears.

Cock a Doodle Do

Jill Haglund

MATERIALS

Rubber Stamps: Rooster by Inkadinkado; Circa 12- pt Rolling Stamp by Provo Craft

Dye Inkpad: India Ink Black by Stewart Superior

Papers: White Cardstock; Natural Pine by Debbie Crabtree Lewis for Provo Craft; Football by The Paper Company

Pastels/Chalks: Portfolio Series Water Soluble Oil Pastels

Other: Paintbrush; Paper Clip

INSTRUCTIONS

1. Stamp image on Natural Pine paper, stamp again on white cardstock in India Ink.
2. Cut a negative mask of rooster from pine paper image. Color the other image with pastels, blend with wet paintbrush.
3. Adhere negative mask over colored image. Tear textured football paper for bottom as shown. Edge card in black ink.
4. Stamp words, cut out, attach with paper clip.

Asian Butterfly Girl

Jill Haglund

MATERIALS

Rubber Stamps: Flowers by Just for Fun; Asian Symbol by Rubber Stampede; Asian Girl with Wings by A Lost Art/Penny Black

Pigment Inkpads: ColorBox Hot Red; Sunshine Yellow; ColorBox Fluid Chalk Powder Blue; VersaFine Onyx Black

Papers: Semi Gloss Cardstock

Pastels/Chalks: Various Chalks

Colored Pencils: Prismacolor

Other: Post-it Notes

Tools: Heat Tool; ColorBox Stylus

INSTRUCTIONS

1. Blend yellow and blue inks onto cardstock with a stylus, dry with heat tool.
2. Stamp Asian butterfly image on top of blended inks. Stamp again onto Post-it; cut out for mask.
3. Cover butterfly image with mask and overstamp with flowers in red ink.
4. Color face of image with colored pencil. Touch up with chalks. Stamp Oriental symbol in red, cut out, adhere.

Wipe Your Paws

Jill Haglund

MATERIALS

Rubber Stamps: All-Night Media/Plaid

Pigment Inkpads: VersaFine Onyx Black

Papers: Cat Tracks by Karen Foster Designs

Paints: Titan Buff and Raw Sienna by Golden

Colored Pencils: Watercolor Pencils; Colored Pencils by Prismacolor

Other: Playing Card

Tools: Bristle Brush

INSTRUCTIONS

1. Stamp cat in black ink, color with Prismacolor pencils. Color paws with watercolor pencil, use water to blend color as shown, cut out.
2. Apply Titan Buff to paper using dry brush technique, add Raw Sienna as shown.
3. Adhere paper to prepared playing card and trim.
4. Add cat image.

Elegant Sisters

Jill Haglund

MATERIALS

Rubber Stamps: Brenda and Brandy Diffusion by Jill Meyer for Hampton Art

Pigment Inkpads: VersaMark WaterMark; VersaFine Onyx Black

Papers: Cardstock

Pastels/Chalks: Various Chalks

Other: Post-it Notes

Tools: Stamp Positioner; Chalk Applicators

INSTRUCTIONS

1. Use stamp positioner to stamp images on cardstock, stamp again on Post-its, cut out for masks.
2. Cover images with masks and overstamp background with VersaMark WaterMark, let dry two minutes.
3. Color with chalks, blend as shown. Lift masks and color images again with chalks.

"C" is for Chalice; "C" is for Chatelaine; "C" is for Crowns, "C" is for Castle

Christy Hawkins

MATERIALS

Rubber Stamps: Chalice, Castle, Queen, Crowns and Architectural Fragment by Oxford Impressions, Magnetic Alphabet Stamps by Making Memories

Dye Inkpads: Memories Black and Chestnut Brown

Papers: Cardstock; Tissue Paper; Crackle Background by Creative Imaginations

Paints: Indian Copper Twinkling H2O's

Colored Pencils: Prismacolor

Markers/Pens: Copper Posh Impressions Accent Pen

Other: Post-it Notes; Metallic Rub-On Copper Kit #1 by Craf-T Products; Antique Brass Pinwheel and Copper Brad by American Tag

Tools: Cosmetic Sponge

INSTRUCTIONS:

1. Cut cardstock to ATC size; cut patterned paper slightly smaller, edge cardstock with copper pen.
2. Stamp image on Post-it Note; let dry, cut out for mask.
3. Stamp image on patterned paper in black ink; let dry.
4. Mask image and stamp background with brown ink; let dry.
5. Color with Indian Copper Twinkling H2O's and Prismacolor pencils.
6. Make a coppery wash over the background with Indian Copper Twinkling H2O's.
7. Sponge Chestnut ink and copper rub-on onto the torn edges; glue patterned paper onto the prepared card, stamp word beside image.
8. Pierce the card and add embellishments.

NOTE: Stamp the queen on thickness of adhered and dried tissue paper in black ink. Tissue paper softens the image and the Prismacolor pencils go onto the paper in an interesting way. Cut out and glue image to ATC

Mah Jong Tile

Dawn Binyon

MATERIALS

Rubber Stamps: Stampers Anonymous

Dye Inkpads: StazOn Timber Brown; Adirondack Ginger; Tim Holtz Vintage Photo

Papers: Brown Mulberry; Glossy Cardstock

Other: Blank Tile; Fibers; Judikins Diamond Glaze

Tools: Dremel; Needle; Decorative Scissors

INSTRUCTIONS

1. Stamp ATC-sized cardstock with image twice. Rub the front of one card with Distress Ink.
2. Use decorative scissors to cut two corners off image stamped on white. Glue to corners of distressed ATC.
3. Edge tile in Ginger ink and stamp part of same image again. Allow to dry.
4. Drill hole with Dremel. Thread fibers through hole with needle.
5. Adhere Mulberry paper to ATC and tile to Mulberry Paper with JudiKins Diamond Glaze.

Alluring Audrey

Lisa Gifford

MATERIALS

Rubber Stamps: Alluring and Audrey Hepburn by The Stampsmith

Dye Inkpads: StazOn Jet Black

Papers: Cardstock; Striped and Dotted Scrapbook Papers

Other: Brads; Transparency Sheet

INSTRUCTIONS

1. Layer striped paper on cardstock and trim.
2. Adhere torn dotted paper, smooth with bone folder.
3. Stamp Alluring on the side of papers.
4. Stamp Audrey Hepburn on transparency, trim to ATC size.
5. Punch holes and attach to ATC with brads.

Bohemian
Carlene Federer

MATERIALS
Rubber Stamps: Hand and Woman by A Stamp in the Hand

Pigment Inkpads: Vintage Photo by Ranger

Dye Inkpads: StazOn Jet Black; Archival Sepia

Papers: Cardstock; Vintage Dictionary Paper by Artists On Collection

Markers/Pens: Burgundy Glitter Pen by American Crafts

Other: Image by ARTchix Studios; Clear Detail Embossing Powders; Small Gold Frame by 7gypsies

Tools: Heat Tool

INSTRUCTIONS
1. Adhere vintage dictionary paper to cardstock.
2. Stamp hand image, heat set with clear embossing powder.
3. Add woman image; place small gold frame over image.
4. Circle word "Bohemian" with pen. Distress edges sepia ink.

Romance
Carlene Federer

MATERIALS
Rubber Stamps: Heart by Memory Box

Pigment Inkpads: VersaMark WaterMark

Papers: Cardstock; Vintage Hip Chic Collection by Making Memories

Other: Image by ARTchix Studios; Gold Super Fine Embossing Powder

Tools: Heat Tool

INSTRUCTIONS
1. Adhere patterned paper to cardstock. Add image.
2. Stamp heart with VersaMark WaterMark, emboss with gold powder, heat set.
3. Computer-generate "romance" and glue to center of heart image.

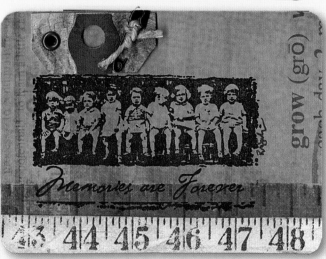

Grow
Roben-Marie Smith

MATERIALS
Rubber Stamps: Ruler, Grow Definition, Children and Script by Paperbag Studios

Pigment Inkpads: VersaFine Onyx and Vintage Sepia

Papers: Scrapbook Paper; White Bond Paper

Other: Coffee-Dyed Tag; Safety Pin; String; Eyelet; Playing Card

Tools: 1/8" Hole Punch; Stipple Brush; Eyelet Setter

INSTRUCTIONS
1. Adhere paper to playing card, stamp images in black.
2. Stamp ruler on white bond paper, stipple to age, adhere to card; stamp definition in brown.
3. Set eyelet in tag, attach safety pin, tie string to safety pin, trim
4. Adhere tag to top of ATC.

Enchant Your Life
Sharon Wisely

MATERIALS

Rubber Stamps: Unmounted Stamps by Red Lead PaperWorks

Dye Inkpads: StazOn Jet Black

Papers: Romani by BasicGrey; Vellum

Other: Metal-Rimmed Circle Tag; Jewelry Tag; Pink Jewel; Heart Eyelet

Tools: Circle Punch; Sewing Machine; Heart Eyelet; Pink Jewel

INSTRUCTIONS

1. Cut cardstock, stamp image.
2. Stamp image on jewelry tag; set heart eyelet in jewelry tag, glue to first stamped image.
3. Cut vellum; trim one edge with scallop scissors; stitch to ATC on three sides to form pocket.
4. Punch circle from cardstock; glue to circle tag, glue pink jewel to center, adhere to top of ATC.
5. Stamp "enchant your life" on cardstock, cut out, glue to ATC.

I Should Think
Lou McCulloch

MATERIALS

Rubber Stamps: Games by Stampers Anonymous; Party Hat Set by Lost Coast Designs

Pigment Inkpads: VersaFine Onyx Black

Dye Inkpads: Adirondack Red Pepper

Papers: Red and White Cardstock

Paints: Red Acrylic

Other: Gesso by Liquitex; Old Photo Postcard

Tools: Stencil Brush; Sandpaper

INSTRUCTIONS

1. Cut white cardstock to ATC size; stamp party hat images on red cardstock in black ink, cut out.
2. Paint white gesso on card; when dry, brush on Red Pepper inkpad with stencil brush.
3. Stamp Games on background, randomly glue on computer-generated phrases.
4. Cut out figures from an old photo postcard and sandpaper edges, glue red hats to figures, paint buttons with red paint.
5. Put two small pop-dots on backs of heads, glue bottom of photo to card and accent with gesso.

Always Play
Lou McCulloch

MATERIALS

Dye Inkpads: Vintage Photo Distress Ink

Papers: Inkjet Fabric Sheets

Pastels/Chalks: Wax Crayons

Other: Cardboard; Vintage Quilt Fabric; Tiny Safety Pin; Mini Buttons by Darice

INSTRUCTIONS

1. Cut stiff cardboard to ATC size.
2. Print out vintage images and words onto fabric sheet and cut out.
3. Cut quilt piece to ATC size and sew small images and words to piece.
4. Sew on small buttons and add safety pin.
5. Attach entire quilt piece with fabric glue to card.
6. Age edges with distress inkpad, add wax crayons if desired.

Chic

Jill Haglund

MATERIALS

Rubber Stamps: Geometric Swirl by Rubber Stampede; Girl with Purse (source unknown)

Pigment Inkpads: VersaMark WaterMark; VersaFine Onyx Black; Vivid! Orange

Other: Black Letters by Paper Bliss from Westrim Crafts; Ribbon; Blue Staples

Tools: Brayer; Stapler

INSTRUCTIONS

1. Stamp swirls with VersaMark WaterMark ink, brayer top with orange ink as shown.
2. Stamp girl image, staple ribbon with blue staple. Add letters to spell "chic".

Little Fairy Babies

Caroline Peeler

MATERIALS

Rubber Stamps: Snowflakes, Script, Alphabets and Phrase (source unknown)

Pigment Inkpads: VersaColor Sky Blue

Paper: Cardstock

Dye Inkpads: Memories Chestnut Brown; Black

Other: Vintage Images; Fabric Scrap

Tools: Decorative Scissors

INSTRUCTIONS

1. Cut out papers, assemble backgrounds, stamp backgrounds and phrases as shown.
2. Cut out desired vintage images and adhere to card, smooth with bone folder.
3. Assemble as shown.

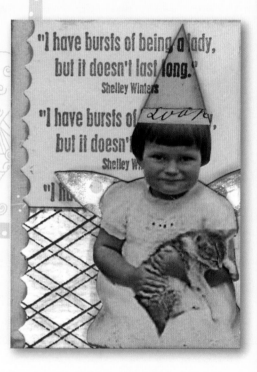

Another Imagination Gone Wild

Jill Haglund

MATERIALS

Rubber Stamps: Dancing Ladies by ERA Graphics; Another Imagination Gone Wild by Rubbermoon

Pigment Inkpads: VersaFine Onyx Black

Papers: Cardstock; Danny O Magazine by K&Company

Colored Pencils: Primsacolor

INSTRUCTIONS

1. Stamp Dancing Ladies on cardstock, color with pencils.
2. Cut out words from Danny O Magazine paper, collage around sides.

Torn Paper Collage

Dawn Binyon

MATERIALS

Rubber Stamps: Playing Card by Eclectic Omnibus; Numbers by Paper Artsy; Text by A Stamp in the Hand; Small Eiffel by A Country Welcome; Mini Solid Dress Form by Invoke Arts; Volute Diagram by Tin Can Mail/Stampa Rosa

Dye Inkpads: Marvy Matchables Dark Brown, Light Brown, Burnt Umber, Ochre, Violet and Cherry; StazOn Jet Black

Papers: Cardstock; Tissue Papers

Other: Image

INSTRUCTIONS

1. Stamp focal image, cut out and glue to ATC. Adhere small pieces of torn tissue paper randomly to ATC. Photo copy ATC.
2. Stamp additional images as shown.

Numbers

Sharon Wisely

MATERIALS

Rubber Stamps: Unmounted Stamps by Red Lead PaperWorks

Dye Inkpads: StazOn Jet Black

Papers: Romani by BasicGrey; Vellum

Other: Metal-Rimmed Circle Tag; Ribbon

Tools: Flower Punch; Sewing Machine; Scallop Scissors; Eyelet Setter; 1/16" Hole Punch

INSTRUCTIONS

1. Stamp image on cardstock in black ink.
2. Cut cardstock for tag and stamp image in black again.
3. Cut vellum; trim one edge with scallop scissors, stitch to ATC on three sides to form pocket.
4. Set eyelet in circle tag; stamp image.
5. Punch flower from cardstock; glue circle tag to flower, pull ribbon through eyelet and glue to vellum pocket.
6. Place stamped tag in vellum pocket.

Another Time

Jill Haglund

MATERIALS

Rubber Stamps: Stampington & Company Block; Splatter Pattern by All Night Media/Plaid

Pigment Inkpads: VersaFine Onyx Black

Paper: Beige and White Cardstock; October Paper by Karen Foster Designs

Paints: Green Acrylic

Pastels/Chalks: Portfolio Series Water Soluble Oil Pastels

Tools: Bristle Brush

INSTRUCTIONS

1. Dry-brush beige cardstock with acrylic paint, then stamp splatter pattern; trim.
2. Stamp woman image, cut out, edge with red pastel. Mat to background paper as shown, edge with black ink.
3. Adhere patterned paper to ATC base, add letters paper. Edge with oil pastels.
4. Attach layered image with foam tape.

Dream
Jill Haglund

MATERIALS
Rubber Stamps: "D" by Stampers Anonymous

Pigment Inkpads: VersaFine Onyx Black; Peeled Paint Distress Ink; Marvy Matchables Carnation Pink

Papers: Cardstock, SK Meadow Stripe by K&Company; Four Block by Anna Griffin

INSTRUCTIONS
1. Crumple Anna Griffin paper, rub paper with pink ink, rub green paper with distress ink.
2. Iron papers flat and adhere to top and bottom of striped paper for card base as shown, stamp letter "D" in black ink.

Time Will Tell
Jill Haglund

MATERIALS
Rubber Stamps: Girl by Stampers Anonymous; Buttons on Background by Paperbag Studios

Pigment Inkpads: VersaFine Onyx Black

Dye Inkpads: Vivid! Stormy Blue; Marvy Matchables Carnation Pink

Papers: White Cardstock; Text Weight Paper

Colored Pencils: Prismacolor

Other: Brads; Old Pink Receipt; Time Transparency by K&Company

INSTRUCTIONS
1. Stamp girl in on text weight paper. Ink edge in pink and mat on receipt.
2. Rub blue directly onto paper, stamp buttons, mat on blue paper.
3. Attach transparency with brads to finish.

Marilyn with Wings
Dawn Binyon

MATERIALS
Rubber Stamps: Wings by Postmodern Design; Manuscript XV by Cherry Pie; Marilyn Monroe by Viva Las Vegastamps; Art Word by Paula Best

Dye Inkpads: VersaMark WaterMark; StazOn Jet Black; Marvy RoseMarie and Orange

Papers: Glossy Cardstock

Other: Bottle Cap; Metal Plate by Making Memories

Tools: Heat Tool; Notched Corner Rounder

INSTRUCTIONS
1. Stamp background manuscript image on cardstock in VersaMark WaterMark, heat set.
2. Rub on Marvy inkpads lightly, buff with paper towel.
3. Stamp remaining images and cut out.
4. Adhere wings image, attach bottle cap and add Marilyn image.
5. Stamp word "Art" on metal plate in black ink, attach with pop dot.
6. Round corners of card to finish.

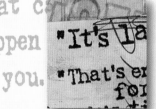

That's Enough Stamping for One Night
Jill Haglund

MATERIALS
Rubber Stamps: It's Late My Love by Catslife Press; Bree by Hampton Art Stamps; Design Element by Stampers Anonymous

Pigment Inkpads: VersaFine Onyx Black

Dye Inkpads: StazOn Timber Brown

Papers: Woodcut Collage Flat Paper by K& Company; Off White Text Weight Paper

Other: Our Story Metal Tab by 7gypsies; Brads

INSTRUCTIONS
1. Stamp Bree, make a mask and cover image. Overstamp with Design Element image.
2. Stamp phrase, tear paper and adhere to ATC as shown.

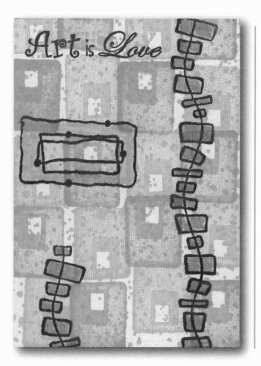

Art is Love

Wayne Dieleman

MATERIALS

Rubber Stamps: Dot and Squares by Magenta; Retro Block by Hero Arts; Pixie Expressions by PSX

Pigment Inkpads: Cat's Eye Rouge Pastel and Yellow Citrus

Dye Inkpads: Ancient Page Coal Black

Papers: White Cardstock

Colored Pencils: Prismacolor

Other: Paintbrush

INSTRUCTIONS

1. Dip paintbrush in Yellow Citrus ink and tip onto cardstock for background.
2. Stamp dots in Rouge Pastel.
3. Stamp retro block in Yellow Citrus and Rouge pastel.
4. Stamp other images in Coal Black. Color several images with pencils.
5. Ink the edges with Coal Black.

Woman's Vision

Wayne Dieleman

MATERIALS

Rubber Stamps: Dots by Magenta; Little Blocks by Hero Arts; Pixie Expressions by PSX; Spiral and Woman by Judikins

Pigment Inkpads: Cat's Eye Blush Rose and Dark Peony

Dye Inkpads: Ancient Page Coal Black

Papers: White and Purple Cardstock

INSTRUCTIONS

1. Stamp dots on white cardstock in Blush Rose ink, stamp spirals in Blush Rose also.
2. Stamp Woman and "Art is Love" in Coal Black.
3. Stamp remaining image in Dark Peony.
4. Cut white cardstock slightly smaller than the purple ATC card base. Glue white cardstock onto purple base.

Journey of the Heart

Wayne Dieleman

MATERIALS

Rubber Stamps: Dots by Magenta; Spiral by Hero Arts; Pixie Expressions by PSX; Lady, Hand and Love by Art Impressions.

Pigment Inkpads: Cat's Eye Blush Rose and Dark Peony

Dye Inkpads: Ancient Page Coal Black

Papers: White Cardstock

Pastels/Chalks: Purple Chalkletts by EK Success

INSTRUCTIONS

1. Color right side of card with Chalkletts.
2. Stamp dots in Blush Rose ink, stamp spiral in Blush Rose also.
3. Stamp Hand, Love and Lady in Dark Peony.
4. Stamp remaining images with Coal Black.
5. Edge card with Dark Peony ink.

Art is Love

Wayne Dieleman

MATERIALS

Rubber Stamps: Dot and Square by Magenta; Retro Stamps by Hero Arts; Pixie Expressions by PSX

Pigment Inkpads: Cat's Eye Rouge Pastel and Yellow Citrus Chalk Inks

Dye Inkpads: Ancient Page Coal Black

Papers: White Cardstock

Colored Pencils: Prismacolor

Tools: Paintbrush

INSTRUCTIONS

1. Dip clean paintbrush in Yellow Citrus ink and tip onto the white cardstock for background.
2. Stamp little dots in Rouge Pastel.
3. Stamp the retro block in Yellow Citrus and in Rouge Pastel. Stamp additional images in black.
4. Color with pencils, ink edges with black.

SWAPS AND ONLINE ATC GROUPS

One of the key purposes of Artist Trading Cards is swapping with other artists. Consider joining an online ATC group. Once you join, you are typically invited to create three or more cards around a theme, such as music, animals, famous people, nature, etc. After mailing off your cards, you will receive the same number in return from another artist. Some artists put a lot of work and time into their cards; others may not. Swappers appreciate when you observe unwritten ATC etiquette by reciprocating with the same quality of artwork.

For a comprehensive list of online ATC swap groups, search the Internet. Below is a list to get you started.

groups.yahoo.com/group/ArtErratica

groups.yahoo.com/group/artisttradingcards

groups.yahoo.com/group/ArtTradingCards

groups.yahoo.com/group/collagecats

groups.yahoo.com/group/FiberATC

www. groups.msn.com

www. heartsart.com

www.amstamps.com

www.artchixstudio.com

www.artellewordsandart.com

www.art-e-zine.co.uk/atc

www.articusstudio.com

www.artist-trading-cards.com

www.Atccards,com/index

www.atcswap.com

www.azcentral.com/home

www.b-muse.com/ATC-Backgrounds

www.cedarseed.com

www.crafty/articles

www.en.wikipedia.org/wiki/Artist_trading_cards.com

www.geocites.com/aussie

www.groups.msnJustLearning/cardswaplist.msmw

www.mailartist.com

www.mailartists.com

www.renmeloen.com

www.scrapbookdesigns.wordpress.com

www.swap.com

www.swap_bot.com/swap

www.thenewgalery.com

www.tracyroos.com

To meet with ATC swappers living all over the globe go to:
www.artisttradingcards.meetup.com

ARTIST TRADING CARD

TITLE

ARTIST

INFO

DATE   EDITION

Artist Trading Card

Title:

By:

Contact:

Date: No:

round robin

round/ rob/in, 1. a sequence or series.
2. a petition, remonstrance, or the like,
having the signatures arranged in circular
form so as to disguise the order of signing.
3. letter, notice, or the like, circulated from
person to person in a group, often with
individual comments being added by each.
4. a tournament in which all of the entrants
play each other at least once, failure to
win a contest not resulting in elimination.

SHOPPING GUIDE

INKS

Adirondack by Ranger Industries
Ancient Page by Clearsnap, Inc.
Archival by Ranger Industries
Brilliance by Tsukineko
Brush Box by Clearsnap, Inc.
Cat's Eye by Clearsnap, Inc.
ColorBox by Clearsnap, Inc.
Dauber Duos by Tsukineko
Distress Inks by Tim Holtz for Ranger Industries
Encore by Tsukineko
Fluid Chalks by Clearsnap, Inc.
Kaleidacolor by Tsukineko
Marvy Inkpads by Uchida
Marvy Matchables by Uchida
Memories by Stewart Superior
Pearlescent by Tsukineko

Posh Impressions by Ranger Industries
Seashells by Ranger Industries
StazOn by Tsukineko
VersaColor by Tsukineko
VersaFine by Tsukineko
VersaMagic by Tsukineko
VersaMark by Tsukineko
Vivid! By Clearsnap, Inc.
Whispers by Sugarloaf Products

PAINTS AND PENCILS

Grumbacher by Sanford
PITT Artist Pens by Faber-Castell
Portfolio Series Water Soluble Oil Pastels by Crayola
Prismacolor by Sanford
Twinkling H2O's by LuminArte

We wish to thank the following companies for allowing us to reproduce their rubber stamp images electronically for the production and design of this book. All images are copyrighted:

Art Gone Wild!
Catslife Press
Hampton Art, LLC
PaperArtsy
Paperbag Studios
Rubbermoon Stamp Company
Stampotique Originals
Stampers Anonymous
The Stampsmith

top secret (tŏp sē krit), adj.

PRODUCT RESOURCE GUIDE

3M/Scotch: www.scotchbrand.com
7gypsies: www.7gypsies.com
A Country Welcome: www.acountrywelcome.com
A Stamp In The Hand: www.astampinthehand.com
Acey Deucy: www.acydeucy.com
American Art Stamp: www.americanartstamp.com
American Crafts: www.americancrafts.com
American Tag: www.americantag.net
American Traditional Designs: www.americantraditional.com
Anita's Art Stamps: Local Craft Store
Anna Griffin: www.annagriffin.com
Ann-ticipations/Stamps N' More: www.ann-ticipations.com
Another Stamp Company: www.anotherstampcompany.com
Appalachian Art Stamps/Appaloosa Art Stamps: www.rsmakers.org
Art Gone Wild & Friends: www.agwstamps.com
Art Impressions: www.artimpressions.com
ARTchix Studio: www.artchixstudio.com
ArtDreams: www.karststage.com/artdreams/
Articus Studio: www.articusstudiodesign.com
Astrobright: Local Craft Store
Autumn Leaves: www.autumnleaves.com
B Line Designs: www.blinedesigns.com
BasicGrey: www.basicgrey.com
Bazzill Basics Paper: www.bazzillbasics.com
Beeswax: www.beeswaxrubberstamps.com
Caran d'Ache: www.carandache.ch
Catslife Press: www.catslifepress.com
Cavallini & Co.: www.cavallini.com

Cherry Pie Art Stamps: www.cherrypieartstamps.com
Claudine Hellmuth: www.lazarstudiowerx.com
Clearsnap, Inc.: www.clearsnap.com
Club Scrap: www.clubscrap.com
Coffee Break Designs: 317-290-1542
Collage Keepsakes: www.collagekeepsakes.com
Colorbok: www.colorbok.com
Coronado Island Designs & Stamps: www.cistamping.com
Crafter's Pick: www.crafterspick.com
Crayola: www.crayolastore.com
Creating Keepsakes: www.creatingkeepsakes.com
Creative Images Rubber Stamps: www.cistamps.com
Creative Imaginations: www.cigift.com
Daisy D's Paper Co: www.daisydspaper.com
Darice: www.darice.com
DecoArt: www.decoart.com
Delta: www.deltacrafts.com
Design Originals: www.d-originals.com
Designs by Reminisce: www.designsbyreminisce.com
DieCuts with a View: www.diecutswithaview.com
Doodlebug Design: www.doodlebug.ws/
Dremel: www.dremel.com
Duncan Enterprises: www.duncancrafts.com
Dymo: www.dymo.com
E-6000 Craft Adhesive/Eclectic Products: www.eclecticproducts.com
Eberhard Faber: www.eberhardfaber.com
Echoes des Voyages: www.echoesdesvoyages.com

Eclectic Omnibus: www.ajsstampworld.com
Eclectic Products: www.eclecticproducts.com
EK Success: www.eksuccess.com
Elf Dust: Local Craft Store
Enchanted Ink: www.enchantedink.com
Endless Creations: www.shopec.com
Ephemera Design Studio: www.ephemeradesignstudio.com
ERA Graphics: www.eragraphics.com
European Papers: http://europeanpapers.com
Faber-Castell USA: www.faber-castellusa.com
Fancifuls Inc.: www.fancifulsinc.com
Fibermark: www.fibermark.com
Fishbone Graphics: Local Craft Store
FoofaLa: www.foofala.com; 1-800-588-6707
Fred B. Mullett: www.fredbmullett.com
Fusion Art Stamps: www.fusionartstamps.com
Gamblin Artists Colors: www.gamblincolors.com
Glue Dots International LLC: www.gluedots.com
Golden Artist Colors, Inc.: www.goldenpaints.com
Great Impressions: www.greatimpressionsstamps.com
Grumbacher/Sanford: www.sanfordcorp.com
Hampton Art LLC: www.hamptonart.com
Heidi Swapp: www.heidiswapp.com
Hero Arts: www.heroarts.com
Hot Potatoes: www.hotpotatoes.com
Impression Obsession: http://impression-obsession.com/
Inkadinkado Rubber Stamps: www.inkadinkado.com
Invoke Arts: www.invokearts.com

Jacquard Products: www.jacquardproducts.com

JRL Design Co.: Local Craft Store

JudiKins: www.judikins.com

Just For Fun: www.jffstamps.com

K&Company: www.kandcompany.com

Karen Foster Design: www.karenfosterdesign.com

Keeping Memories Alive (KMA):
www.scrapbooks.com

Krylon: www.krylon.com

Leave Memories/Blockhead Stamps:
www.blockheadstamps.com

Leavenworth Jackson: www.ljackson.com

Li'l Davis Designs: www.lildavisdesigns.com

Limited Edition Rubberstamps:
www.limitededitionrubberstamps.com

Lindy's Stamp Gang: www.lindystampgang.com

Little Lace Lady: www.littlelaceladyshop.com

Loew Cornell, Inc.: www.loew-cornell.com

Lost Coast Designs: www.lost-coast-designs.com

LuminArte Inc.: www.luminarteinc.com

Lyra: www.lyrapencils.com

Ma Vinci's Reliquary:
http://reliquary.cyberstampers.com

Magenta: www.magentastyle.com

Magic Mesh: www.magicmesh.com

Making Memories: www.makingmemories.com

Marvy Uchida: www.uchida.com

McGill, Inc.: www.mcgillinc.com

me & my BIG ideas: www.meandmybigideas.com

Me and Carrie Lou: www.meandcarrielou.com

Meer Image: www.meerimage.com

Melissa Frances: www.melissafrances.com

Memories Complete: www.memoriescomplete.com

Memory Box: www.memoryboxscrapbooking.com

Modern Masters, Inc: www.modernmastersinc.com

Mostly Animals: www.mostlyanimals.com

Museum Stamps: www.museumstamps.com

My Sentiments Exactly: www.sentiments.com

Nick Bantock: www.nickbantock.com

Ninji: Local Craft Store

Non Sequitur Art Stamps: www.
nonswquiturstamps.com

Northwoods Rubber Stamps: www.
northwoodsrubberstamps.com

NRN Designs: http://nrninvitations.com

Old Town Crafts: www.oldtowncrafts.com

Oxford Impressions: www.oxfordimpressions.com

Paper Inspirations: www.paperinspirations.com

Paper Source: www.paper-source.com

PaperArtsy: www.paperartsy.co.uk/

Paperbag Studios: www.paperbagstudios.com

PaperWhimsy: www.paperwhimsy.com

Paula Best and Co. Rubber Stamps: www.
paulabest.com

Pebbles Inc.: www.pebblesinc.com

Peddler's Pack Stampworks: www.peddlerspack.
com

Penny Black Rubber Stamps:
www.pennyblackinc.com

Plaid Enterprises, Inc.: www.plaidonline.com

Portfolio Series: www.portfolioseries.com

Post-it Notes/3M/Scotch: www.scotchbrand.com

Postmodern Design: 405-321-3176

Postscript Studios: Local Craft Store

Prang: www.prangpower.com

Prima Marketing, Inc.: www.primamarketing.com

Printworks Collection:
www.printworkscollection.com

Provo Craft: www.provocraft.com

PSX: www.psxstamps.com

Ranger Industries, Inc.: www.rangerink.com

Red Lead PaperWorks:
www.redleadpaperworks.com

Reminisce: Local Craft Store

Renaissance Art Stamps: 860-485-7761

River City Rubberworks:
www.rivercityrubberworks.com

Rose Art: www.roseart.com

Rubber Baby Buggy Bumpers:
www.rubberbaby.com

Rubber Dub Dub:
www.rubberdubdub.safeshopper.com

Rubber Gems: www.rubbergems.com

Rubber Soul: www.rubbersoul.com

Rubber Stamp Tapestry:
www.rubberstamptapestry.com

Rubber Stampede: www.rubberstampede.com

Rubber Stamps of America: www.stampusa.com

Rubbermoon Stamp Company:
www.rubbermoon.com

Rusty Pickle: www.rustypickle.com

Sakura of America: www.sakuraofamerica.com

Sandi Miller Art Stamps: www.usartquest.com

Sandylion Sticker Designs: www.sandylion.com

Sanford: www.sanfordcorp.com

Scenic Route Paper Company: www.
scenicroutepaper.com

Sharpie: www.sharpie.com

Shrinky Dinks:
www.shrinkydinksgoemerchant7.com

Sissix: www.sissix.com

SkyBluePink: www.skybluepink.com

Sonburn, LLC: www.sonburn.com

Sonnets Studios: www.sonnetsstudios.com

Staedtler: www.staedtler.com

Stamp Camp: www.stampcamp.com

Stamp Francisco: www.stampfrancisco.com

Stamp It Up: Local Craft Store

Stamp it!: www.stampit.com

Stampa Rosa: www.creativebeginnings.com

Stampabilities: www.stampabilities.com

Stampendous: www.stampendous.com

Stampers Anonymous:
www.stampersanonymous.com

Stampin' Up!: www.stampinup.com

Stampington & Company: www.stampington.com

Stampland: www.stamplandchicago.com

Stampotique Originals: www.stampotique.com

Stamps Happen, Inc.: www.stampshappen.com

Stewart Superior: www.stewartsuperior.com

Sugarloaf Products: www.sugarloaf products.com

Suze Weinberg: www.schmoozewithsuze.com

Tamarind: Local Craft Store

The Card Connection: Local Craft Store

The Cat's Pajamas Rubber Stamps:
www.thecatspajamasrs.com

The Moon Rose Art Stamps:
www.themoonroseartstamps.com

The Paper Company: www.paperco.co.uk/

The Punch Bunch: www.thepunchbunch.com

The Queen's Dresser Drawers:
www.thequeensdresserdrawers.com

The Stampsmith: www.stampsmith.net

Toad Hall/Rubber Anarchy: www.amstamps.com

Tombow: www.tombowusa.com

Tracy Roos: www.tracyroos.com

Treasure Cay: 727-784-0880

Tsukineko: www.tsukineko.com

Twinkling H2O's: www.luminarte.com

Uchida/Marvy Uchida: www.uchida.com

Uptown Rubber Stamps/Uptown Design Company:
www.uptowndesign.com

USArtQuest, Inc.: www.usartquest.com

Viva Las Vegastamps: www.vivalasvegastamps.com

We R Memories: Local Craft Store

Westrim Crafts: www.westrimcrafts.com

Willow Bead: www.craftdiner.com

Xyron: www.xyron.com

Zettiology: www.zettiology.com

Paris In My Soul 2006

SONG

You Can Always Spot A Lady

LADY BUGS

oh happy day

Bird Eggs-Plate 12

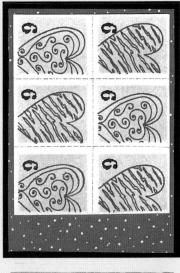

MINE

Coffee: Water with an attitude!

·Percy·

If we can't laugh at ourselves,

let's make fun of someone else!

New York Gallery, 28 Third St. S. F.

JOURNEY

EXPRESS

EXPRESS

EXPRESS

nation unknown

destination unknown

Nature does nothing uselessly ·Aristotle·

Feather.
s. d. main stem; d. calamus
or quill; s. rachis: r. c. c. barbs
cut away on right side in order
not to interfere with view of b.
the aftershaft, the whole of the
left web of which is likewise cut
away.

6

1000
LIST OF
APPLICATION
COOPER CYCLES